ROCK YOUR COMEBACK

ROCK YOUR COME BACK

THE DOWN-TO-EARTH GUIDE TO RECLAIMING YOUR POWER

NICHOLE EATON

publish
your gift

ROCK YOUR COMEBACK
Copyright © 2023 Nichole Eaton
All rights reserved.

Published by Publish Your Gift®
An imprint of Purposely Created Publishing Group, LLC

Printed in the United States of America

ISBN: 978-1-64484-626-1 (print)
ISBN: 978-1-64484-627-8 (ebook)

Special discounts are available on bulk quantity purchases by book clubs, associations and special interest groups. For details email: sales@publishyourgift.com or call (888) 949-6228.
For information log on to www.PublishYourGift.com

Camryn and Kylie—every piece of work in my life will be dedicated to you, the little girls who turned me into the person I was meant to be. This book is to remind you it's safe to be yourselves. You can always return no matter how far away you get from your light. You are so freaking loved. Move through the world with a strong mind and soft heart. Every inch of you is magic.

"I wanna thank me for believing in me. I wanna thank me for doing all this hard work. I wanna thank me for having no days off. I wanna thank me for being me at all times…You a bad mother**ker."

—Snoop Dogg

INTRODUCTION

INTRODUCTION

My preschool class pet was a beige and white hamster named Buttons. Buttons was your typical classroom pet: he ran happily on his wheel, lapped water from his drinking tube, and munched on seeds and nuts.

The best part? Buttons had a clear ball that allowed him to run freely around the classroom, bumping into the chair legs as if competing on some obstacle-course television show. *Buttons would've kicked ass on the show Wipe Out.* Our entire class was thrilled to have our very own pet. Considering I didn't have my own pet at home, I was extra ecstatic.

Each weekend was a chance for a lucky classmate to take Buttons home. When my designated weekend finally arrived, I gleefully gathered his crate, his magic freedom ball, and Buttons' adorable furry self, whisking him off to my two-story home on 10th Street in a small Upstate New York town.

We were a match made in hamster heaven. Buttons was just as stoked to be in my home as I was to have him. Holding him up, I showed him around, explaining that the sunroom was under construction. I turned on all of the lights for him because, well, he couldn't reach. I was certain he was just as scared of the dark as I was. We snuck into my sister's room so he and I could giggle at her New Kids on the Block shrine. Buttons loved my room the most. He, too, was a huge Holly Hobbie fan.

In the evening, I helped my mother with dinner, putting Buttons in his plastic ball so he could run wild and free through the open-concept kitchen and dining room. After dinner and getting ready for bed, I tucked him into his little home. He nested into the wood shavings and fell fast asleep. That night I dreamt about Buttons, hoping he was also dreaming about me.

The next morning, I excitedly raced downstairs to reunite with our furry house guest, skipping the last few steps by sliding down the banister. I opened Buttons' cage...to find him completely still.

Y'all, I killed Buttons.

After first screaming at the top of my lungs for my mother to do frantic Hamster CPR, I realized his poor little body was stiff, and no amount of tummy pushing was going to make his tiny heart beat again.

Take five seconds to imagine stepping back into pre-K on Monday morning and being the kid who killed the class pet. Although I will defend myself by saying my teacher determined he died of natural causes! I like to believe it was simply the rush of excitement from the perfect night before, and he died a happy little hamster.

After failing to convince my mother to invest in a Buttons impersonator, I graced the classroom with my presence, hoping the words "hamster murderer" wouldn't be engraved on my forehead. I was sad. I was guilty. Maybe I'd fed him too many snacks? I prepared myself for a day full of angsty classmates and refused to make eye contact with anyone for a solid week.

Many of the kids were sad. Some cried. My poor unexpecting teacher was forced to give an impromptu lesson on death and dying. And although I had been fully prepared to defend my non-hamster killing, grieving self, at the end of the day, I didn't need to. A few kids in the classroom wouldn't play with me at recess, but other than that, life went on. As it does.

Now, what does this have to do with comebacks? I'll tell you. For my young self, pre-school had made its mark as my very first incident to come back from.

A comeback is traditionally tied to the sports player or entertainer who comes out of retirement. But in this book, a comeback is the reconnection to your inner voice allowing you to come back to who you inherently are. The one who knows you can have more, feel more, and be more. It's the activation of your authenticity, your deeper truth, especially after a period when you've felt broken, lost, or stuck. Your comeback is an alignment of your thoughts, beliefs, and actions. A spark of imagination to dream up who you're capable of becoming. It's a compassionate dismantling of every bullshit inner story keeping you from being happier. Your comeback will amplify your inner strength, intuition, and creativity. In your comeback, you will remember who the fuck you are: a force, an extension of the Universe, and most importantly, the designer of your best life.

How do you know you need a comeback? Oh, you'll know. But in case you're not sure, here are some clues: When the things that once brought you joy no longer do. If you've gone through loss, breakup, layoff, or any major life change. When you've simply started to recognize the path you've chosen, the personality you've identified with, isn't fulfilling or doesn't "feel right" anymore. And as my friend, author of *Not Another Diet Book*, Heather Maio, says, "When you're no longer okay with living a life that feels just okay."

This book is both for those currently in a dark place and those who are just feeling like life could be better but aren't sure where to start. The truth is we never know what challenges life will bring us. This book is equipped to meet you wherever you're at.

Our journey on this earth is filled with highs and lows. Our job is to use the lessons from the lows to become a better version of ourselves. As author Marshawn Evans Daniels wrote in her book *Believe Bigger: Discover the Path to Your Life Purpose*, "Disruption is the invitation." Chaos is a time to reconnect with yourself. It's an invitation to step back into your power or into a better version of yourself.

Coming back to yourself is the key to success. It's not about never getting knocked down in the first place. You would have to hide in your parents' basement with a lifetime supply of Cup o' Noodles to avoid life's valleys. Even then, I'm sure the Universe would send in a tsunami or some other disaster to push you out of your comfort zone.

Showing back up to your life or rebuilding yourself after you feel like your world has been burnt to the ground is about knowing you're worth coming back to. There's so much possibility left. Resurrecting yourself can be challenging, but I promise you it's possible.

Whatever has been weighing on your heart that has you breaking into pieces, whether a big move, a big loss, a rejection, a tragedy, or a disease, I'm telling you right now, you can come back from it. You are not stuck. You are not lost. You are not weak. You are not damaged or broken. You are a damn miracle. You are an extraordinary power. You are the Universe wrapped in a meat suit. *Gross, but accurate?*

I promise you that no matter how far you've gotten away from yourself or your power, I will give you the mindset shifts and tools necessary to rise back up better than before. Each part of this book helps with a different aspect of your comeback. The different parts work together, building and combining different ideas and skillsets.

The Part in the Dark will help you manage the tough emotions and understand the purpose of challenging times. The Part Where You Question Everything will help you examine perceptions, beliefs, and patterns of behavior that may be keeping you stuck. The Part Where You Undo will give you actionable tools to start changing your mindset. The Part in the Light will help you understand the role of the Universe, energy, and intuition in your transformation. Lastly, the Part Where You Create will give you the actionable steps to combine the power of the mind with the power of the Universe to shift your energy toward creating a life you love and becoming the best, most powerful version of yourself.

That's the goal of your comeback, after all: stepping fully into who you were always meant to be. Making choices that feel aligned and in your highest good. Feeling that you control your life, rather than it controlling you.

Oh, by the way, I'm Nichole! I'm a master's-level mental health counselor who has mastered my intuition. I take a unique approach to help clients change their minds and reactivate their souls. I've spent over a decade working with people one-on-one to show them their power, reconnect them with their authenticity, and help them hear and trust their intuition. I'm obsessed with neuroscience yet equally gripped by the mystical and magical. I've been up close and personal with the deep truth, vulnerabilities, and challenges of being human. If there's one thing I know well, it's people.

I deeply believe in practicing what I preach, and I know these practices I'm about to share with you are life-changing. I know this because they've changed my life, too. They've pulled me out of some of the darkest places that I lovingly refer to as black holes.

This book is what I needed to hear in each phase of my personal comeback. I've compiled the practices I know work and the reminders that have not just helped my clients but also morphed me into the person I am today: a recovering people pleaser who now sets boundaries and stands unapologetically in her truth. A person who was once crawling out of her skin with insecurities to someone who is confident and sure of herself. A young mom who went from receiving government WIC checks to be able to feed her baby to someone who now has enough abundance to help others. Most importantly, a woman who was buried knee-deep in her own depression to a woman who is now deeply, genuinely happy. I've learned how to love both myself and the life I live.

You get to change your life in whatever way you feel called, too! I promise to teach you from every angle how to step back into your power, be more yourself, and feel more alive than you have in a while.

I'd be doing you a major disservice to not tell you all my secrets. *I don't gatekeep.* Whatever you're up against, I know that with your resiliency and inner strength, combined with my masters in mental health and spiritual expertise, together, we're unstoppable!

PART 1.

THE PART THAT
FEELS DARK

A comeback seems a little dramatic, doesn't it? Maybe you're reading this like, "Nichole, I'm not 2001 Michael Jordan coming back to the NBA." Perhaps your life isn't as messy as Britney Spears's was circa 2007. Or maybe it is. Maybe life as you know has gotten turned upside down, or maybe it's just been a hot minute since you've felt like yourself. Either way, this is the perfect time for you to get your shit together and take your life back into your own hands.

Overcoming isn't cute. It looks more like a toddler left unsupervised for forty minutes with their mother's makeup bag. But I can promise you that the part where it feels dark has a purpose. We will uncover it together, make a game plan for what I call "black hole moments," clean up the internal mess, and neutralize the heavy feelings. This part is about holding compassion and gaining understanding. I pinky promise to give you actionable tools throughout the rest of this book to get you back on track to living your best life.

We all have our own moments in the dark where we aren't our happiest, best selves. Some moments in the dark are mild and short-lived, and some are downright horrendous. Every single person on this planet has their own unique black hole experiences that shape their lives and personalities. It's necessary that we don't compare our hard times to the hard times of others.

Depression and anxiety are your soul's check-engine lights. Feeling over-stressed, lonely, disconnected, or stuck all the time? That's the way your soul throws up the Bat Signal when you're driving on empty. Sometimes our soul needs to be loud AF because it's been cluing us in for months (or even years), and we haven't paid attention. When we neglect all our warning signs, the Universe steps in to shake things up.

Although I don't always understand what the Universe is doing when bad things happen, I know something for sure: Rock bottom is the foundation for the most intense comebacks. You might not have seen that something needed to shift in or around you, but the Universe did.

Maybe you're still unsure what needs to change to make you happier. I know the feeling; what I call black-hole moments can be scary. I promise that together, we can work through hard feelings to remind you of your power. Because what I know for sure is that your power is always there. Let me show you.

Chapter 1:

BLACK HOLE MOMENTS

You are the alchemist of your life. You might have been presented with shit, but I'm going to teach you how to turn it into gold.

But first, I want to talk about black hole moments. Aftermath moments. The ones that shake you to your core and make you question yourself, your life, and whether the Universe even exists. You lose a job, the big project you invested in flops, or the person you love leaves. These are paralyzing moments of disbelief and shock your body doesn't even know how to process. I refer to these as black hole moments because what we know about black holes is that things get sucked in and don't return.

We've all had those seasons where we've felt stuck in a situation or a feeling that we can't see our way out of. It feels confusing that everyone else's lives are swirling around at a normal pace while ours have just stopped dead in their tracks. The black hole moments are scary. They feel like they don't have a chance in hell at ending. There's an overwhelming refrain of "How the hell am I ever going to feel better?"

At that moment, you can't envision it for yourself. You can't imagine this heartache alleviating. You can't foresee moving through life without being consumed by longing or sadness.

The scariest thing about the black hole moments from the times I've experienced them is that life feels pointless. Our bodies are often catapulted into survival mode. Our goal in those helpless, hopeless times is to stay alive, even if that means taking baby steps to get where we are going.

A black hole moment always requires three major steps.

1. Walking through your black hole

2. Alchemizing your black hole

3. Making meaning in your black hole

Walking Through Your Black Hole

For us to walk through our black holes together, I'd first like to share mine. Have you ever had a time in your life where there was a distinct before and after? A season where you can look back and say, "This is where everything changed"? Mine was the summer of 2007. At nineteen, I got married and moved to a new city to pursue my bachelor's degree. This was the first time I had lived over an hour away from all my friends and family. I was nervous yet excited to start a new school with new people and fresh opportunities. However, after a few weeks in our new apartment, I discovered I was unexpectedly expecting just a couple weeks after my twentieth birthday.

In all honesty, I cried for weeks. This wasn't part of my plan. I had never even held a baby. How was I supposed to be someone's mother? How was I supposed to finish school or follow the big dreams I had for myself? My vision for my bright future began to dim.

That same summer, my parents ended twenty-four years of marriage. A week after finding out about my pregnancy, my mother moved a thousand miles from our family home in New York to Florida. Within two months, everything I knew as normal and had identified as "home" was upheaved. My entire life felt foreign. I was now a twenty-year-old, married, pregnant college student whose parents lived a thousand miles apart.

The chaos landed smack dab in the pursuit of my bachelor's degree. Professors strongly encouraged me to drop their courses, telling me I couldn't be successful in their classes while pregnant. But I stayed, and I passed.

Nine months passed, and 8 pounds, 6.9 ounces later, I realized my life would never be the same. After I gave birth to our daughter, Camryn, we struggled. I'd love to say it was just in adjusting to being new parents or standing in the upright position without being in immense pain, but struggle seeped into every part of my life. My new normal consisted of showing up to school on three hours of sleep and pumping breast milk in a bathroom stall during every break.

Being a student and a young mom made me feel like an outsider. Finding common ground in conversations was a challenge. What did I have to talk about outside of how little I slept last night, how I forgot to pack wipes in the diaper bag, or the mastitis I had developed? No one could relate. Friends stopped inviting me to parties because I could never go. People fail to mention that having a baby changes everything about your social world. It can be incredibly isolating. They also fail to mention that when you become a mom, taking care of yourself or prioritizing your needs often comes with guilt.

My carefree, sunshine personality seemed to disappear under immense responsibility. How was I suddenly responsible for a whole other living, breathing human when I was still figuring out how to live on my own and take care of myself? Who was I outside of the new roles of being a mother, wife, or student? I found myself just going through the motions, watching with jealousy as my childless friends partied their way into turning twenty-one.

On top of my sense of self deflating, we struggled financially. I don't know if you've ever put your child in daycare, but it's freaking expensive. In order for me to finish school and for my husband to work, we had to prioritize paying for childcare. My husband's job at the time was commission based. He worked twelve-hour days with a two-hour commute. During this season of our lives, we had only one income. After paying out daycare, some weeks, we would have enough to catch up on bills.

Other weeks, we would have to prioritize which utility was more necessary just in case one got shut off.

Everything felt hard all the time. Even our relationship, which had always felt light and easy, started to feel tense and distant. I was spread thin, over touched, and overwhelmed. I still don't really know if it was postpartum-related or circumstantial, but I slipped into a vicious depression that made getting out of bed a challenge. This time period was one of my darkest black holes.

I found myself on autopilot, just surviving. Joy felt like a pipe dream. My days consisted of waking up, going to school, coming home, taking care of the baby, and going to bed, only to do it again the next day. The more my days repeated themselves, the worse I felt. Was this bound to be my existence? Was everything I wanted for myself now out of reach?

I'd love to say this was short-lived, but the truth is depression consumed me for years. Camryn was two when I found out, in the heat of my master's degree, that I was pregnant with my second little girl. I delivered Kylie one week after graduation.

Although this sadness and struggle felt never-ending at the time, a year or so after I had Kylie, something in me began to shift. I was exhausted from being exhausted. This couldn't be the life I was meant to live, could it? This wasn't the mother these little girls signed up for. I decided to be willing to believe that this wasn't all there was for me. That I needed to get my life and myself back. And slowly but surely, one day at a time, I did.

I began to deep dive into the power of the mind and an understanding of who I was in connection to the Universe. In unlocking my personal power, everything began to shift.

I wish I could go back and show the twenty-year-old version of me, sobbing over the sink, pregnancy test in hand, the life we live now. She wouldn't believe me. I would tell her that we would be more than okay. That we would end up being a pretty great mom. We'd finish school with a 4.0 and own two thriving businesses. We would have the opportunity to help thousands of people from all over the world. *And write a couple books in the process.* I'd let her know we'd have more than enough abundance to not only feed our family and keep our lights on but to help others in need. I would tell her that happiness wasn't a pipe dream. That the hard would alchemize into something great and that those little girls would change us in every way possible for the better. I would let her know that to have the life we have now, that summer had to be the turning point of it all.

Black holes aren't pointless. They have a function in our growth. Hard times unlock personality traits, resources, and relationships we didn't know we needed. Eventually, in time, we may even come to be grateful for these challenging moments. *It's definitely okay if you can't imagine being grateful at this moment.*

The good news is black hole moments don't last forever. Yours and mine included. The important part of moving out of the dark hole isn't deciding at that moment *how* it has to happen because it won't feel clear. In survival mode, we can only see what's directly in front of us. So, you don't need to decide *how* you will get out. You just need to decide that you *will.*

When we decide that we will do something, our brain begins to look for possibilities of how to make that happen. It searches internally and externally for proof and pathways. Your willingness alone is a brilliant and powerful first step out of the dark. It opens up routes for a shift in your mindset, which will lead to a shift in your emotions and behaviors. *Baby steps.*

In black hole moments, one day can feel like a million years. In this heavy energy, it's necessary to decide just for today; you will just wake up and get through it however possible. This is vital because black hole moments *do* shift! They slowly start to alleviate. The depth and the intensity can't last and eventually neutralize. Until then, focusing only on what you want today to look like is a way to make it feel more manageable. This technique is popularly used in twelve-step programs. *It gets to get better.*

Focus only on your healing. Only on the basics. Maybe just for today, you wake up and shower. Maybe just for today, you set a couple of goals that feel good to you. Perhaps it's as easy as promising yourself you'll drink a full glass of water when you wake up. And then, actually doing it. Maybe just for today, you try a yoga class. Maybe just for today, you focus on taking a deep belly breath every time your mind starts to get chaotic.

My story didn't end with the struggle. Yours won't either. Everything is temporary. Seasons are temporary. Emotions are temporary. This is such great news for us. We know we've been through hard stuff before and have found our way back.

Each day, decide you're open to believing there's more for you, that you deserve a beautiful life. Each day you wake up, decide your life gets to get better, and slowly life can improve. Start by choosing to be open and willing to see things differently. A new perspective. A shift in perception.

Start to envision what it might be like on the other side. How might you feel on the other side of this chaos, healed up and in your best light? What would you wear? What would you act like or think about? Maybe it can be easier than you thought. Maybe getting to the other side is more possible than you imagined. What if your comeback doesn't have to be hard? What if we just take it one day at a time?

If you're in a black hole moment, recognize that the darkness doesn't last forever. Be willing to believe there's more for you. Use the phrase "just for today" every day. Focus your attention and intentions on what you can work on or control today and today only. Begin to envision what the best version of you looks like, acts like, and wears. Let's decide right now and together: not only will you shift out of this darkness, but we will let it be easier than you could have ever imagined.

Alchemizing Black Holes

I once watched a video of a news anchor unknowingly biting into the hottest pepper in the world, a Carolina Reaper. Almost immediately, the man began to panic, sweat, and turn bright red. His mouth was on fire, and he began gagging into the microphone. The Carolina Reaper produces some of the most intense side effects, leaving its victims in pain for hours after ingestion. Eating the wrong pepper, like our black hole moments, can be all-consuming. Luckily, even with such an intense reaction, what we know about hot peppers is there is a way to neutralize the spicy effects: milk!

The good news is that even big, heavy energy can be neutralized. How do we neutralize this powerful energy? We stop feeding it. It's like seagulls on the beach. You see one, think it's cute, and feed it a potato chip—two minutes later, you've accidentally summoned thirty temperamental, squawking seagulls ready to shit all over your beach setup.

This doesn't mean we won't ever acknowledge or think about the bad thing that happened. It doesn't mean we don't ever say, "Hey, I'm in this crappy black hole, and I can't see anything but darkness." I'm not into avoiding our darkness. That's called positivity bypassing, and healing doesn't come from pretending everything's fine all the time. We are capable enough to face it. But we need to refuse to let it consume us.

I highly suggest finding a therapist, a good friend, or a group—someone safe to talk to about the situation. Try to limit the amount of time that you spend talking about and focusing on it outside of this designated space. Remember, the more we feed the seagull, the more seagulls will show up. The more we think about something, the more similar thoughts and evidence for those thoughts show up.

Create a designated time and place once a day or once a week to give yourself permission to focus on the problem at hand. Psychologists call this worry time. Give yourself permission to ruminate. Whether it's an hour or just fifteen minutes, in that time, you can be as crazy-obsessive as you want. You can process, explore, understand, and "figure it out."

Now that you have this beautiful healing, talking, thinking time carved out, any time you start worrying, thinking, or obsessing about the issue, I just want you to notice you're doing it. Catch yourself going down the spiral staircase of thoughts. I don't even care if you start having awareness after half a day of accidentally ruminating on your problem. Start wherever you notice. We are going to begin to train the mind to listen to us instead of just running the show. The techniques later in this book will help you train your brain and disrupt old thinking patterns. But for now, just notice. *Baby steps.*

Whenever you catch yourself thinking about the situation and recognize it's not helpful to you, I want you to take a deep breath in and just focus on where the air goes in your body. Follow the flow of air in through your nose, down through your lungs, and back out. Any thoughts that pop into your head while breathing, just acknowledge them and return your focus to where the flow of air is in your body. See if you can make this next breath slower and fuller. Fill up your belly and expand your rib cage. Make the next breath even slower. See if you can give the following breath a color. What color would calm be? What color is your higher self's energy? Breathe it in. Follow the flow of air down through your lungs and back out. As you exhale, give the crappy energy and negative feelings a color. What color can we breathe out and release? Is it a murky brown or a drab gray color? Where does this heavy energy sit in your body? Breathe it out.

What we are doing with this technique is neutralizing the energy. We are stripping the momentum of the thought simply by not feeding it. By placing your attention back on you and what's in your control, you design the "now" moment. We are flowing air through our body and oxygenating our brain to make it work better and be more powerful. We are dictating our focus rather than getting hijacked by its old familiar routine.

As we practice this technique, we become better and better at it. Doesn't it feel sort of silly that simply breathing, the natural, automatic thing we don't even realize we do half the time, can be such a vital piece to creating a stair step out of the black hole? *See, I told you this could be easier than you thought.*

Your job is to breathe. That's it! Just breathe. Just follow the flow of air. When you start feeling that yucky energy get big, just breathe. When you start feeling over-whelmed, just breathe. Let it be slow. Let it be easy.

Neutralizing a black hole is one of the best ways to start shifting out of it. You can begin by catching your-self when your thoughts start to gain momentum. You can also create a time to worry. Remember: Focusing on breathing is like milk to a hot pepper: the best neutralizer.

Making Meaning in the Black Hole

A close friend of mine was recently going through a breakup. She was deep in a black hole moment. This was someone she had been planning on spending her life with. He had told her she was not the right fit for his fu-ture. She found out a week later that he was seeing some-one else. Devastated, her meaning-making brain began comparing her devastation with how happy he must be. How this girl he was seeing must be superior in some way. How she was over here, a total train wreck, and he was in love, living his best life.

Now, remember, she hadn't spoken to him since the breakup. She had no idea what was true. She was filling in the gaps based on her own fear-based stories, which was creating a landslide of negative feelings. The truth of the matter was he had felt her pull away and was trying to make her jealous. He wanted her back. He confessed this a few months later. *Don't worry—she didn't take him back.* Instead of filling in the gaps with assumptions or projections, remind yourself you don't know the full sto-ry. It isn't helpful to guess.

While we work toward acceptance, we have to remember our brain is a meaning-maker. I talked a *ton* about this in my first book, *Rock Your Soul: The Down-to-Earth-Guide-to-Mastering-Your-Mind.* Your brain tries so hard to make meaning out of scenarios. According to a June 2020 article from Wu Sai Neurosciences Institute at Stanford University, "Our brains unconsciously bend our perception of reality to meet our desires or expectations. They fill in gaps using past experiences."[1]

The mind attempts to fill in gaps when we don't have all the details. The danger in our brain filling in those gaps is it doesn't typically fill in the gaps in your favor. In fact, it's more likely to fill in the gaps with bullshit stories based on our self-worth, self-perception, or personal fears.

Instead of "I didn't get my dream job because of some unknown factor like timing or nepotism," I start making this rejection about not being good enough, smart enough, or experienced enough. When we begin to predict what might have occurred based on our own self-perception, we create stories that typically have no weight or truth to them. We end up making ourselves feel worse and prolong our healing process.

Someone once told me thoughts that feel bad are usually bullshit. Truth usually feels good or, minimally, a neutral knowing. When we start filling in the gaps of perception with our own stories, we use these gap fillers as evidence against us. Our brains provide fake evidence that not only impedes our progress but makes us feel small and unworthy in the process.

We don't know what we don't know. It's vital to ask yourself, does this mean you've made a bad self-worth-based prediction? Is the ego using this prediction to keep you from moving on, to keep you small, or hold you back from stepping into your power? A story to keep you from healing? Ask yourself if the stories you're creating around the event are even true.

We can also acknowledge that maybe my friend wanted to be further along in her healing journey before she learned the news about the new woman. But comparing where we are to where we "should" be only creates more issues to come back from. "*Shoulding*" ourselves creates guilt and shame rather than action. Eliminating this word can be helpful in your healing journey. "I should feel better by now" is a lot different than "My priority is to create habits and surround myself with people that help me feel better."

I just want to remind you of our intention. Remember, we've decided we *will* get through this, and it will be easier than we thought. Which means we have to call ourselves out every now and then. We have to get clear on our words and if we are using them as weapons *against* our growth or in *the promotion* of our healing.

What if, instead of meaning-making, we try accepting the situation as it is? My favorite acceptance affirmation is, "I don't know why this happened, but I accept that it has, and I choose to be willing to move forward."

You can create your own affirmation that feels good or empowering.

Some of my personal favorites include:

- "I accept that which I cannot change and choose to refocus my thoughts on what I can."

- "I surrender my control and wait for the lesson to be revealed."

- "I focus my energy on things in my life that do feel good and release the rest."

- "I am open and willing to redirect my energy and focus."

Our brain always wants to figure out *why* something occurred, but sometimes the *why* works itself out way after the fact. It might be that the *why* isn't clear until ten years down the road. So, you don't have to know *why* this happened. You just have to stop fighting that it *has* happened.

When we resist what occurred by trying to figure it out or fight it, we are feeding the seagulls again. We are searching our environment for evidence or proof that what happened isn't our reality and that the circumstances are not what they seem. By accepting our reality and situation as is, we cease growing its power. From acceptance, we can start rebuilding.

I want to acknowledge distraction as a healing tactic before the end of this section. However, I won't promote chronic distraction! Staying busy after something that feels catastrophic will absolutely catch up to you if you are trying to run from your problems. But I do suggest that in the beginning, there are moments you will feel sucked so deep into the black hole that choosing to distract yourself from your thoughts by doing yoga, listening to upbeat music, or learning about something new is a great way to neutralize the energy so you can alchemize it.

You can figure out where you are in your healing process by paying attention to your thoughts, mood, and energy. Heavy energy typically equates to a bad mood and challenging thoughts. I like to think of it as a scale. Are you feeding the bad mood with your thoughts, feelings, or actions? Are you neutralizing the heavy energy through breath, distraction, or acceptance? Are you moving forward with the energy by designing a future? Check in with yourself right now and see what part of the scale you're on.

What Mood Am I In?

What type of thoughts are creating my mood?

Good Mood

Joy/appreciation/love

"I am so grateful for the experience and what it has taught me."

Passion/enthusiasm/optimism

"I'm hopeful this situation can turn around."

Hopefulness /contentment/boredom

"I accept what has happened. I wonder what is next for me."

Pessimism/frustration/overwhelment

"I keep trying but it doesn't seem to work."

Dissapointment/Doubt/Worry

"I am so bummed it didn't go how I wanted it to."

Anger/Revenge/Jealousy

"Everyone has what they want except me. It must come easy to them."

Insecurity/Fear/Depression

"I just feel so hopeless. Nothing is going my way."

Adapted from the Emotional Guidance Scale
created by Abraham Hicks

Black hole moments can be scary, but they aren't permanent. Your job is to neutralize them by not making meaning out of the situation that impedes your progress. Ask yourself if what you believe is true or helpful. You can follow the emotional scale to help you choose thoughts that will shift you into a better mental state and mood. Accept and neutralize to begin the process of truly moving forward.

Chapter 2:

WHEN IT GETS UNCOMFORTABLE

Change happens in one of two ways. It's either thrust upon you without your approval, or you create it. For those of you who aren't currently in a black hole moment and might just be uncomfortable, this part is for you.

I've always felt like there's a very distinct moment in every person's life. I call this noticing. It's the sudden awareness that whatever you are doing, whoever you're with, or wherever you are located on a map doesn't *feel* right.

The annoying thing about noticing is it's not always based on logic. In fact, most of the time, it's the opposite of logic. That swanky Vice President chair suddenly gets harder to sit on despite the money in your bank account. Your long-term relationship suddenly feels stale even if everything is stable.

The best way I can talk about discomfort is to tell you about the time I went out for a run with my pants on backward. *Bear with me.*

A few years back, I regularly ran three to five miles several times a week. One morning, I threw on my favorite pair of basic black yoga pants and set out for a run. These pants were my very favorite ones. *You know, the kind of pants so comfortable you don't feel like you are wearing any?* The booty-shaping, fit-like-a-glove, love-handle-hiding ones? *Those ones.*

Three miles in, my favorite pants were failing me. I was ready to rip my hair out due to the amount of readjusting I had to do. I was so uncomfortable. It was then I realized that my pants were, in fact, on backward. *I had gotten dressed like a toddler this morning.*

My run turned into a walk. The more uncomfortable I felt, the more annoyed I became. I couldn't take it anymore. I realized I had a choice in front of me.

I could keep experiencing discomfort.

Or

I could squat behind a bush down a side street in broad daylight and change my pants around.

If you're wondering what I did, go ahead and picture me, pants down around my ankles, squatting behind a bush.

When I think of the big noticing moment in our lives, it's a lot like running with your pants on backward. Noticing something isn't quite right or isn't fitting you the way it used to may take a while. You may be going along with your day and have this sudden feeling that something needs to change. You may have the realization that you've just been putting your left foot in front of your right for the past decade without knowing where you're going or why you're going there.

Once you notice, it's hard not to notice. Noticing gives you two choices: make a shift or stay in your little (*dis*)comfort bubble. If you choose to stay in your comfort bubble, the Universe will likely begin shifting life around until you feel even more uncomfortable. The Universe may even amp it up a bit, taking your previously comfortable job and giving you a new boss who is a raging jerk. Your boyfriend, to whom you once felt so close, starts acting shady and distant. Little problems will surface, not just internally but in your external world.

Let me be clear, the Universe doesn't do this because it hates you, although there have been times in my life I've been strongly convinced otherwise! Discomfort occurs because we very rarely grow in comfort. Most people don't take their life to the next level unless what is directly in front of them truly isn't working.

Discomfort is a weird way the Universe shows you that there's more out there. More happiness. More love. More success. More excitement. More money. Bigger opportunities. More, more, more—all for you!

Change has been on my mind for the past few years. I decided in 2018 to pack up my life, my husband and two little girls, and move 700 miles away from New York and everything I had ever known, including friends, family, and even my thriving intuitive therapeutic business that I owned with my best friend, Christy. *Yes. This is exactly as terrifying as it sounds.* From an outsider's perspective, my move must have looked like I closed my eyes, threw a dart, and landed in South Carolina. This wasn't the case.

A year or two prior to moving, I started feeling really restless. All the things that had once felt aligned and exciting suddenly started to feel off. I determined that I had no real reason to feel this way, so I pushed through in hopes life would eventually shift back to normal. It never did. These uncomfortable feelings kept growing to the point that I was forced into major soul searching. I began to explore what I felt like I was missing. I started asking the bigger questions like "What do I really want?"

I began traveling constantly. At this point in time, I still didn't have much money, so I day-tripped anywhere less than five hours one way. I couldn't plan my next trip fast enough. I became obsessed with escaping. Every weekend, especially in the summer, I drove to new cities, hiked new mountains, and visited new waterfalls looking for solace from the discomfort I was feeling. Although these adventures provided temporary relief, upon returning home, the excitement of the day would fade, and I'd be backfilled with restlessness.

I spent that New Year's Eve visiting family in South Carolina. I had been down to visit many times over the past decade, and every time it felt harder to leave. I'd arrive back in New York feeling homesick for a place that wasn't my home. On that particular New Year, there was something about waking up to 70 degrees, sunshine, and a day full of playing outside with my kids. I was so happy to the point of tears. At that moment, I realized all the travel I'd felt I needed was actually my soul pulling me to explore other areas to call home.

Awareness of the need for change and an actual decision to follow through are two separate things. At the time, moving both my and my husband's established businesses and uprooting our kids seemed far-fetched. Most people who are born in our small hometown stay in our hometown. But the intuitive nudge that I didn't belong in New York anymore stayed steady, despite my fears about moving.

The following August, my husband and I impulse-signed a lease while visiting the Carolinas. We packed up our house and left New York in the dust by November. We were so excited about all the new opportunities. Excited to live near a thriving city. Optimistic about the impact I could make on this new community. Over the moon for the weather, beach proximity, and all the things!

Five weeks into the move, the excitement was replaced with a feeling of being invisible combined with deep-seated loneliness.

I missed my friends. I missed social activities and walking into a place where everyone knew me. I called one of my best friends and asked, "Do you think I made a mistake?" She replied, "Of course I'd love for you to come back, but I've always admired your ability to take big leaps and follow your heart. If your heart and intuition called you there, I think it's important to wait and be open to seeing what the Universe wants you to learn or experience."

In the midst of all my excitement, it wasn't that I hadn't weighed the odds of what I was losing. I just hadn't given myself time to grieve. Moving was my choice and the right choice. But I had felt forced to fake happiness for my friends, family, and clients who missed me, even if I wasn't yet.

The reality is when you make a massive life change, you are losing parts of your normalcy and routine. You might lose connection with people or parts of yourself. It's okay to be a little jacked up about that. Give yourself time to grieve any and all changes. Have compassion for the adjustment period.

I've put together a few things that helped me feel better about change in my life. I hope they help you feel better about changing yours, whether you're considering a cross-country move, leaving your job to dive into a self-owned business, exiting a relationship, adding a child to your family, or any other major life event.

Find Hope

If you didn't choose the change and the change chose you, I'll simply say I don't always understand the Universe, but I deeply believe the Universe doesn't happen *to* you; it happens *for* you. Trust and believe that your life can continue to grow and evolve in a positive direction.

If this was a change you did choose, hold your vision for what you know is possible for you. Know that in time, you will readjust. You're capable of figuring it out. If you're like me and have less patience than my late grandma playing Bingo, then this is a perfect place to practice patience instead of trying to control the situation. Maybe you need to up your prayer count. Set a few more intentions.

Focus on the Present

As much as it's fine to give yourself time to grieve, *you can't stay there.* I began to find little things to get excited about in my new hometown, whether it was meeting new friends, attending yoga at local breweries, finding delicious new restaurants, or discovering cool art galleries. I looked for joy in small moments, like soaking in the sunshine. Breathe and bring yourself into the present. How are you going to become your best self in this new scenario? What's something you've always wanted to try or do?

Raise Your Standards

Guess what? Change is a perfect place to reassess. You get to stop accepting what has been normal and demand a better life for yourself. We can get way too comfortable accepting less than what we actually want in our life. We habituate letting people treat us poorly and rarely ask for more.

In this change, however, you can shake everything up. Go through and see what you really want. What types of relationships do you prefer? How do you want people to treat you? What is your ideal job setting and co-worker situation? What kinds of people or friendships do you want to surround yourself with? You get to decide.

Know Yourself

The post-move period gave rise to a lot of reflection. Life changes really show you what you're made of and what parts of you need strengthening. It's okay to hide out a little and take a few extra bubble baths. It's totally fine to read more self-help books than ever. This is a great time for learning, uncovering, and reflecting. Ask yourself the hard questions. Get to know who you are and what you like. *Fire back up your badass self-worth.*

The thing I know about myself is I've been through some shit. I've survived losses, traumas, and betrayals. As hard as it was, or as low as it made me feel, there's one thing I know for sure: I have always come out on the other side stronger and better than before. I believe that to be true about you, too. If you *decide* it is.

If you are on the edge of something, just swimming in discomfort—if your mind has wondered what else is possible for you—let it. Awaken your curiosity. More *is* possible for you. Stepping back into the driver's seat of your life is doable. Give yourself time, refocus, hold hope, keep your vision, and ask all the important questions. And I hope that if you have a choice between sitting in discomfort or changing your life, you squat behind a bush in broad daylight and change your damn life.

Chapter 3:

PURPOSE IN THE LOW POINTS

My early twenties were spent working as a group counselor for a domestic violence shelter. I saw terrified children with their battered and bruised mommas grace the doors of the home daily. One woman in particular—I will call her Jody—had been back a few times over the span of the year. She was extremely intelligent, kind, and patient with her kids. But sadly, she was involved with a very toxic partner.

The last time Jody came into the shelter, she looked at me with two black eyes and a very swollen lip and sincerely said, "I can't keep doing this." There's always a moment with clients where I can feel the genuineness of a decision. That declaration was the moment she decided to forge a new path, never looking back. Sometimes we are doomed to repeat old patterns until our soul knows we are finally done.

A few years later, Jody wrote an email to me to share that she had moved a thousand miles away from her toxic situation. She had built a brand-new life. Jody now speaks all over the United States as a domestic violence awareness advocate. She assists in training teachers, police officers, and social service employees in recognizing signs of domestic violence. But most importantly, Jody found her happiness and her strength once again. She found healing and peace for herself and her kids.

I'd prefer life without valleys. I'd like to wake up knowing my day was going to be perfect. Zero chance of hardship or heartache? Sign me up! But I've yet to see someone get far in life without being taken out or challenged by something significant.

Life's low points create some of the most magnificent growth within us. Darkness unlocks pieces of us we never knew we had, uncovering both strength and resiliency. Tough experiences give us one hell of a story to share. Our purpose often gets revealed when the lights are off. My point is not solely that we must encounter valleys but that we *need* valleys.

Our purpose can become clear to us while hitting rock bottom. Hard times encourage new choices and carve new paths. Settling is easy. Staying in a job you hate even if it sucks is easy. Our brain prefers the comfort of the known, even when what has been predictable doesn't feel good.

The bottom is often the perfect place to shake up old patterns or ways of existing. Tough times beg you to step into your truth. They are a catalyst inviting you to stop shrinking. Challenges have a funny way of stripping away the bullshit you've acquired to impress people. They pose the question: *Who are you really?*

All magnificent transformations require pressure, a complete undoing of the original form. Take a seed, for example. A seed is buried in the darkness, then asked to wait. The seed has deep potential for greatness. What if it lost sight of the flower it could be while it was waiting in the dark?

The reality is our seed might be in the dark for a while. Under the earth, she will slowly unravel. This seed will fall apart—she has to. Insides of the seed spill out uncontrollably until the day it blooms. But when she blooms? Look out, world. She will bear fruit while spending the rest of her time soaking in light. Could you imagine if the seed wasn't planted at all? Or give up from being in the dark too long? She would completely detach from her potential.

There is no fruit without that initial darkness. There is no wine without the crushing of the grape. There is no diamond without pressure. Darkness has a way of shaping and molding you. Dark times are how the Universe upgrades you.

If you're currently the seed, staring at the dark all around you, understand this is your planting. You have to stick around to see the fruit. *Baby steps.* Sunlight is coming. Your planting is your soul's unraveling. Know there's a purpose here. There are parts of you unlocking for your next level.

Chapter 4:
BACK TO THE BASICS

A few years back, my daughter brought home a cabbage plant from school, whom she lovingly named Mr. Cabbage. Her class had been challenged to see who could grow the biggest cabbage plant. The day she brought it home, we had a frost. Obviously, Mr. Cabbage needed to wait to be planted. I set the cabbage in the room with the most sunlight. I closed the door to ensure our cat wouldn't have Mr. Cabbage for lunch—and promptly forgot about it.

A week later, I could not figure out what terrible smell was permeating my house. If you're a parent, you recognize this as an "oh shit" moment. Running into the sunroom, I saw Mr. Cabbage's sad, wilted leaves flopped over my windowsill, pathetically staring at me. *I just killed my daughter's school assignment.* The smell of cabbage death lingered for a whole week. *Talk about a Buttons flashback when I had to email the teacher to explain.*

When we are in turmoil or far away from ourselves, we can forget about basics: sleep, fueling our body with healthy foods, drinking water, fresh air, and sunlight. As

41

we learned from Mr. Cabbage, without attention to our basics, we will struggle to thrive.

Maslow's Hierarchy of Needs is one of those pyramid theories you learn in psychology class—not to be confused with a pyramid scheme. This layered pyramid suggests that in order for humans to feel intrinsically motivated to reach each next tier of their personal growth, they must be stable in the lower tiers first.

What acts as a barrier to feeling loved, developing healthy connections, or building self-esteem? According to Maslow, our very basic physiological and safety needs comprise the bottom two tiers and, ideally, should be met before we can fully move up into our best selves.

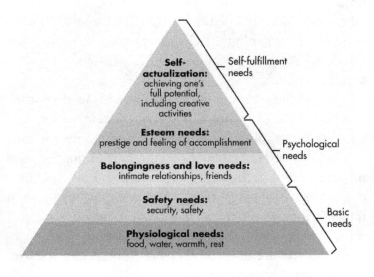

This isn't to say people can't create a great life without these tiers fulfilled; we know the stories of homeless overcomers like J.K. Rowling and Halle Berry. But if you're going through a lot, intentionally stabilizing the bottom tiers may help you prioritize and move up to a better feeling quicker.

When we are in a dark spot, we typically lack the consistency of the bottom layers of the hierarchy. For example, losing our job might cost us nights of sleep and cause feelings of uncertainty. Our safety is threatened, and we don't know if we will be able to feed our families or pay the rent this month. How do we truly step into the best version when we aren't eating or sleeping?

It makes sense that after a major loss, doing more than just surviving feels hard. Maslow definitely says it is! For all of us dying to move on with our lives, or to all the friends telling us to "get over it," Maslow says you *can't* fully until you go back to the basics.

Transformation is set to be an intentional time period but also a bit of a selfish one. You have to put gas in your tank in order to drive any further in your car, which means we have to hone in on the basics before we can invite love and optimism back in. The following are areas to consider tending to when you're beginning your comeback:

Get Some Rest

What are you doing to ensure a good night's sleep? Sleep is an essential reset to not only the cells that are responsible for our physical healing but also our mindset. The

Sleep Foundation suggests that each phase of sleep helps with important brain functions like better thinking, learning, and memory, along with boosting emotional and mental health.[2]

According to neurologist and sleep study specialist with Sutter East Bay Medical Foundation Joanna Cooper, M.D., device screens, like your cell phone, stimulate the part of the brain that suppresses the production of melatonin.[3] An increase in melatonin helps our body not only fall asleep but stay asleep. Limiting screen time prior to bed may help your natural melatonin levels increase.

A few other options for getting a good night's sleep include keeping a consistent sleep schedule by going to bed at the same time nightly. Getting exercise during the day can also help you feel more ready for bed in the evening. Try meditation or hypnosis from YouTube as you fall asleep. I'm a huge Jason Stephenson and Michael Sealey fan. To keep the phone light at a minimum, I like to put my headphones in, turn my phone brightness down, and flip my screen face down.

Another option is to soak in an Epsom salt bath with lavender oils. Salt, in general, helps clear energy. Combining a warm relaxing bath with an energy cleanser is a powerful combo for a good night's rest.

Food as Fuel

For me, personally, energy is required to feel most like myself. A lack of energy just makes me want to hide under my comforter and sleep. Fueling my body has become an important practice not only for my energy but for my mental health.

In fact, more and more studies have emerged to showcase just how essential our food choices are to our mental health. Gut health expert Dr. Amy Shaw suggests that 95 percent of serotonin and 50 percent of dopamine, our happiness chemicals, are made in the gut, suggesting we can vastly improve our mental health by reconsidering our diet.

An August 2020 article based on the aggression of Australian male prisoners showed a 30 percent decrease in violent misconduct following a switch from traditional prison food to a nutrient-based diet and multivitamins.[4] Are the foods you're consuming making you more irritable? Knowing the effect choosing better food can have on our minds and moods makes eating healthier more pressing. Are your foods fueling you or messing with your mood?

Another consideration to make when entering your comeback phase is the amount of protein in your meals. Protein has been proven in several studies as a major player in our focus and concentration. During times of stress, your body requires more amino acids to regulate your central nervous system. Amino acids are found in proteins. To help your brain function optimally, improve focus and concentration, elevate mood, and manage stress, proper protein intake can play a small but vital role. A Harvard Health blog suggests the best way to figure out how much protein to get is by multiplying your weight by 0.36.[5] For example, someone who weighs 150 pounds will benefit from at least 54 grams of protein daily.

Changing the way I eat has been a journey for me. I have made it easier on myself by keeping my kitchen stocked with healthy options like proteins, veggies, and fruits. You can romanticize eating healthy by spending a Saturday morning at your favorite farmer's market. Eat at home more often than you eat out. Find healthy breakfast or lunch staples to ensure that at least one to two meals per day are good for you. Try new Pinterest recipes. Trade out that second cup of coffee for hot water with lemon and honey. Pay attention to your energy levels and mood before and after you eat so you can make better choices. Up your protein intake. If we know we can help our healing process through the foods we choose, why would we not choose better for ourselves?

Water

Are you exhausted, or do you just need more water? Water helps our body function at its best. Did you know that being properly hydrated impacts our memory, attention, and energy according to a June 2019 article in *the International Journal of Environmental Research and Public Health*?[6] Researchers studying dehydration's impact on cognitive functions showed that we are more likely to feel foggy, confused, or fatigued when we aren't drinking enough water. Not only that, but hydration assists our digestive tract, circulation, and muscles, improving our overall energy. Be intentional about starting your day with a glass of water. Carry a water bottle with you everywhere you go. If you notice you're feeling off, foggy, or tired, use it as a sign that you need to up your water intake.

Move It

Movement is essential for your mental, emotional, and physical health. It's one of the best ways to clear your energy and reduce stress.

Did you know that when we are working out, our brain shifts into something known as transient hypofrontality? Researcher Arne Dietrich says this is just a fancy way of saying exercise gives the thinking part of your brain a rest, allowing other areas and functions to become more dominant.[7] This may enhance creative thinking, problem-solving, and feelings of being in the flow.

Go for a walk. Have a dance party. Join a yoga class. Give your body a good shake. Commit to a workout program, even if it's just from home.

Sun and Earth

Let's not underestimate the importance of fresh air and vitamin D. Neuroscientist Andrew Huberman suggests that ten to thirty minutes of safe exposure to sunlight on our eyes in the morning can profoundly impact our mood, health, and hormones.[8] *Yes, that means you have to temporarily ditch the sunnies.* Sunlight is an energy booster, but vitamin D also plays a role in mental health. In the 2010 scientific article, "Vitamin D and Depression:

Where is all the Sunshine?" researchers suggest that effective detection of low vitamin D levels in depressed patients is shown to improve quality of life and long-term health outcomes.[9] Spending intentional time taking in sunlight in the morning works wonders for your soul and your body. I encourage clients experiencing depressive symptoms to get tested for vitamin D deficiency. I'm a huge advocate for functional medicine.

When we were cavemen, our bodies were charged naturally by the earth's magnetism. Although the earth's magnetic field has weakened over time, we can still be intentional about utilizing it to recharge our cells. *The Earth is basically like a people charger.* We call this grounding. Our cells reset themselves by walking on the earth. *Bonus points if you're barefoot.*

A study by Oschman, Chevalier, and Brown shows that grounding helps reduce inflammation in the body, improves sleep, reduces pain, regulates our nervous system, and reduces stress.[10] You can get additional grounding points by gardening, hiking, or walking in the woods.

Eliminate

Back to the basics means being conscious about how you're spending your time. Eliminate what no longer serves you. Clean out your closet or donate to a local shelter. This also means clearing people, habits, or even items around the house. Take an inventory of how you're spending your time. Create a time log by jotting down how much time you spend on each activity throughout the day, including little things like answering texts, social media, and even brushing your teeth. You may even choose to keep a time log for a full week to get clear on where you are spending the majority of your time and energy. Weed out what's working and what's not.

Our environment, clean or messy, can also impact our mental health. Tidying up or cleaning can help us feel clearer, more focused, and energetically lighter. Your external space is often a reflection of your internal space. You can create more clarity and confidence by picking up your space. Start with one small section at a time. Maybe this looks like putting away that load of laundry or tackling the stack of papers on the counter. Set a timer for five minutes to start.

Unplug

Throw your phone in the ocean. *Kidding, don't.* But our phones have become a problem, pulling our energy from the present moment, placing demands on us with texts, depleting feelings of connection, and invoking comparison through social media.

Aim to shrink your screen time. Put your phone in a drawer when you get home for the day. If you can't completely shut it off, consider sleeping with your phone in another room. *Yes, traditional alarm clocks do still exist.* Unplugging from tech may help you feel more creative, purposeful, productive, and hopeful.

Connection

Ditching social media gives way to healthy in-person connections. Reconnect with people who make you feel like anything is possible. People who do not judge you or what you love. People who will listen but not allow you to stay wallowing in self-pity. People who are down for some fresh air and sunshine. Seek out friends who leave you feeling better than they found you. No close friend group? No worries! Seek out a Meetup group in your area. Try a class or volunteer.

Become intentional about committing to your basics. *Baby steps.* Make a personal promise to get better sleep tonight or drink more water today. Following through on one small promise to yourself a day can improve your sense of self-worth and self-trust, leading you on the right path to stabilize those bottom tiers of the hierarchy. Get outside and get rid of what doesn't feel good. Unplug from your phone and plug it back into your soul. Although we will deep dive into more mental and energy tools later, starting with the basics is a great first step to your comeback.

Back to the Basics Checklist

- ☐ Did I get enough sleep?
- ☐ Did I drink enough water?
- ☐ Did I move my body today?
- ☐ What's a healthy dinner option?
- ☐ Do I need to clean my space or get rid of anything?
- ☐ Am I in need of in person connection?
- ☐ Did I get outside?

yes!

PART 2.

THE PART WHERE YOU QUESTION EVERYTHING

Nothing changes if everything stays the same. Imagine if we were all still rocking white eyeliner and JNCO jeans. Tell me you didn't think that looked hot in the early 2000s! *You can't.* In retrospect, we can recognize that overplucking our eyebrows and wearing jeans under dresses were faux pas. But at the time, we didn't know.

At some point, though, we realized it wasn't a good look. As a culture, we were able to learn from these horrific mistakes.

Making your comeback means understanding that the way you've always done things might not be as sexy as you think it is. This part of the book promises to help create genuine awareness when it comes to changing your life. Together we will assess what works and what doesn't. We need to explore what has happened, what we believe about it to be true, and most importantly, what meaning we have created from it. Have you decided your life will never get better? What have you decided your past means for your future?

Undoing comes with recognizing people, situations, and ways of thinking that no longer work for you. It's time to examine parts of the story you've created that block you from reaching your potential. Sometimes to move forward, first, we must look back. Undoing is the pathway to creating a new life.

Chapter 5:

THE RETURN FROM NORMAL

During the 2020 lockdown resulting from the COVID-19 pandemic, the nation got hooked on a docuseries called *Tiger King*. *Tiger King* gave an inside look at the wild lives of exotic animal owners and zookeepers.

The series drew fascination and amusement due to its anything-but-normal scenarios and characters. The world couldn't stop watching or talking about it.

The gun-toting, sequin-wearing, tiger-owning, wanna-be politician and gay polygamist Joe Exotic created a cult-like experience for his employees. His staff was composed of ex-cons and wanderers who had been lured in by big cat appeal. Workers were placed in living conditions crawling with cockroaches. Dinner was made with expired meats.

This was horrifying to the docuseries viewers, but it was normal for the workers living in these conditions. Their working and living conditions had been subpar for so long that the zoo employees had acclimated. Getting your arm gnawed off by a tiger at work might be substantially different from how they grew up, but over time, it had become commonplace. Their brains thought it was typical.

On a smaller but more personal level, when my youngest daughter was six, she had a pair of light-up sneakers with which she was obsessed. She refused to get a new pair because she loved her light-up ones so much. After noticing a growth spurt, I finally forced her. Sliding on her new pair, she said, "Wow, Mommy, my toes are stretchy." I had no idea what she meant until she showed me that her too-small shoes forced her to scrunch up her toes. With shoes that fit better, she could actually stretch her toes out.

The same is true for our lives. Sometimes we live so long in a situation that shrinks us. We simply adjust to it. Typically, people around us can see it, but we're blinded from seeing how non-normal our normal is. Just because you've adapted to your circumstances and have developed measures of getting through it doesn't mean the situation is healthy or aligned with your best self.

Whatever your normal life, behaviors, or thinking looked like prior to this transition, it's okay to miss or grieve it. Big shifts like job changes, location changes, and losses of relationships may have left you feeling like your life feels foreign. Part of moving forward comes with the acceptance that what was your normal is no longer your normal. And the good news? You get to create a new normal.

I think even when life is going smooth as eggs, there's always a chance you've neglected something. For example, some of us can get blissful in our relationships and end up neglecting important friendships. Or it's easy to become so absorbed in our work that we work ninety hours a week, losing touch with our partners or kiddos.

First things first: There must be an acceptance that your old life isn't coming back. When pursuing your comeback, I want you to be careful about falsely believing that coming back means going back. Back to how things were before, back to the job you lost, or back to the relationship that left.

Coming back is a return to who you are on the inside, but it isn't going back to the former external situation. It's moving forward into no place you've ever been before because you're different now. Darkness changes us. In order to move forward, Oprah says, "we must be willing to give up the hope that the past could have been any different." Acceptance of where you're at evolves you. Your new life will require an upgraded 2.0 version of yourself.

Creating a new normal is like upgrading your phone or computer. Learning a new system or way of being may initially feel odd, frustrating, or tricky. Maybe even unnatural. The new program could have troubleshooting or glitches involved. It may feel foreign to you. You might pine for the times when you only had to click the mouse once to keep things running properly. But then you realize the new shortcuts are making your life easier, solving problems you didn't even know you had. I can promise you if you're willing to give it a chance, the 2.0 version of you is worth the upgrade.

Upgrading isn't a discard of who you inherently are. We want to keep what we love, what we're proud of, and what we've learned. We are going to enhance and shape what's working. Then we're going to make small shifts to what isn't until you feel aligned and more like yourself than ever before.

We are creatures of habit. Prehistorically, familiarity had an important purpose. What was known was safe. Venturing into the unknown as a caveperson put your physical safety at risk to other tribes or dangerous animals. Although we no longer need to worry about our physical safety to the extent our caveman ancestors did, we still find ourselves getting stuck holding on to the familiar out of fear.

Just because it's familiar doesn't mean it's working for you or who you desire to be. Just because you've always abandoned yourself for the sake of others, been a people pleaser, hidden from your worth, or pushed people away doesn't mean it's serving you or leading you to what you ultimately want.

You're worth unlocking all the next levels of yourself. You're like a Transformer. All of the pieces are inside of you to morph you into a better version of yourself. *Or a badass earth-saving autobot.* Tough times? That's where the resiliency and personality features to blast you into your best self get unlocked. To truly upgrade, we have to go through our internal system and see how we arrived here.

Take a look at what was normal before. Be willing to give up the belief that there's only a familiar way to live your life. Shifting into a new place in your life may feel foreign, but I promise you it's worth it. Being open and willing to believe new norms can feel just as great if not better.

Chapter 6:

SELF-ABANDONMENT

When I was eleven, my aunt Kim, thirty-two, was killed by a driver who was experiencing a psychotic break and intentionally trying to kill people. Chaos followed her passing. Because her death was deemed manslaughter, there were months and months of court cases and news interviews. My grandma lived with us at the time. After two adoptions, Kim was her first biologically born child, a miracle after being told she would never conceive. When Kim passed, I watched as my grandma morphed into a sobbing shell of herself.

I spent much of my time after Kim's death cheering my grandma and the rest of my family up. I learned quickly to alleviate the heaviness in the room by becoming whatever anyone wanted or needed me to be. At the drop of a hat, I could be the jokester, the entertainment, or the empathetic shoulder to cry on. I became so concerned with everyone's needs and balancing other people's emotions that it took me three months to really cry about the major loss.

I started shifting the truth at a really young age. I don't mean that if I got caught scribbling with purple crayon on the walls, I'd deny it was me. I mean that I learned from a young age when someone asks you how you are, you say "good" or "fine." I learned the polite response was not to burden anyone with your bad days or bad thoughts. I was a chameleon who molded myself into the version of me that the other people in the room wanted or needed. Truth shifting is the gateway drug to self-abandonment.

When I was sixteen, I learned that the best way to keep my feelings to myself was with pot brownies and a casual three to four Smirnoff Ices. I was by no means the poster child for bad kids. I was good, kind, and on the honor roll. To the outside world, including my family, I was perfectly fine. *Because, obviously, that's what I was telling them.*

In my constantly slightly buzzed reality, I was absolutely not fine. My soul was begging for someone to hear it, but all I could mutter were words like, "No, I'm okay."

I was brilliant at forgetting what I needed. If I didn't acknowledge that I had wants and needs, they simply ceased to exist, right? As long as everyone was happy, I was happy, too. Right?

This way of functioning is known as self-abandonment. It involves neglecting our own needs and instincts for the approval or prioritization of others. Signs of self-abandonment may include codependency, people pleasing, over-achieving, feelings of insecurity, second guessing yourself, perfectionism, being overly self-critical, and not trusting your instincts.

Why do we, as humans, especially women, feel societal pressure to lie about how we are, who we are, and what we want? A 2010 study showed that self-scrutinizing and people-pleasing as coping styles are more prevalent in women (54 percent vs. 40 percent in males).[11]

Somehow, I internalized the message that I was needing too much, wanting too much, taking too long, and taking up too much space. So, I tried to be smaller and quieter. In high school, some might have considered me damn near invisible.

This lasted well into my early twenties. After having kids, life felt hard. I maintained the practice of stuffing down all my deepest thoughts, needs, and desires. I was a mom now. I was just going through the motions of taking care of everyone and everything. Who even has time to think about real wants and desires?

Self-abandonment is derived from limiting beliefs. A limiting belief is a repeated thought that keeps you stuck and keeps you from changing your life. I had a limiting belief that moms were only there to make their kids happy. The old adage goes, "If they are happy, I'm happy." What I know now is that this isn't true or necessarily healthy. Yes, we want the kids to be happy. But we also want to model to them how to be happy even after they are done being kids. Plus, our happiness and independence are important, too!

During this time of believing that moms were essentially just self-sacrificing creatures who weren't allowed to have real needs or independence outside of their families, waves of depression frequented my day. Abandoning yourself doesn't feel good. More often than not, denying your needs, feelings, and emotions creates feelings of anxiety, indecisiveness, and low self-esteem. We also may find ourselves in unhealthy relationships where we aren't valued or treated with love.

Returning from self-abandonment comes with reprioritizing yourself. Creating a designated time in your day that is solely for you. That could be sitting in the car an extra ten minutes before scooping the kids up from daycare. It may look like waking up a little earlier to get your workout in or having a quiet cup of coffee while reading your favorite book. Reprioritizing may also mean that you cut down on extra activities to create time. Be willing to step down from the board you're on. Be open to the kids only doing recreation ball instead of travel leagues.

Coming back to ourselves means tuning back into how we are feeling and what we are honestly thinking about our life or situations. You may start with a morning or nightly check-in with how you're feeling, how the day went, and what you need. The first step is just identifying. The next is to create the time to be intentional about meeting your needs. Look to your back-to-the-basics checklist for clues on where to start.

As you regain your focus to include yourself, being kind and compassionate to yourself is necessary. This may look like speaking kindly to yourself. Monitor self-talk that is critical and judgey. Claiming your comeback starts with treating yourself like you are someone you love and value. How do you treat others you care about? How do you speak to them? What if you were your own best friend?

As you strengthen your inner voice, there will also come the point where you begin to vocalize your wants or needs. You may feel called to stand up for yourself or set a boundary. Don't worry if you're not sure how to do this. I have an entire chapter dedicated to boundary setting to help you feel more confident.

Recovering from self-abandonment means we are improving our trust in ourselves. Be someone you can count on. If you say you will do something, make sure to do it. Our brain builds confidence every time we follow through on what we say we are going to do. Set yourself up for success by making little promises to yourself. This may mean setting up a time to check in with yourself and ensuring you take the time to do so or simply taking your hand, placing it over your heart, closing your eyes, and just tuning into your soul self.

Remind yourself that you, too, are worthy of love and belonging. Remind yourself that your voice is valuable and important and that it matters. Making your comeback is about bringing that inner world back to life by honoring it and cultivating it. You deserve to be heard. You deserve to be loved. You matter. You are worth it.

Begin by recognizing when and where you are leaving your true feelings behind and putting yourself last. Step into your day with the intention of treating yourself with love. Create mindful moments throughout your day and time for yourself to reflect. Be kind to yourself and compassionate about where you are at. Monitor the way you are speaking to yourself. Follow through on the promises you make to yourself. Every moment is a chance to start over.

Chapter 7:

THE TRUTH WILL
SET YOU FREE

At twenty-two, I found myself in my very first therapist's office. She sat there in perfectly pressed pants, one of those really nice shirts with a Peter Pan collar, and fancy-looking loafers. She was a strong woman; I could immediately tell. She was honestly kind of scary, giving off a whole Judge Judy vibe. I realized she was the type of woman who asked for what she wanted and probably was going to make me do the same thing.

Remember, at this point in my life, I was a sleep-deprived, head-down new mom just trying to get through graduate school for counseling. My husband worked a million hours a week at a commission-based job. We were lacking in the friend and social life department and were lonely. Oh, and we were can't-keep-the-lights-on broke.

Despite all of that, you would've never known. My day-to-day was filled with smiling, doing, completing, and perfecting. My Instagram pictures portrayed a successful put-together person and an adorable little family.

Back in my therapist's office, my palms were Eminem-level sweaty. I wiped them, then immediately asked her about her day. When she returned the conversation to me, I flawlessly switched our topic to the weather.

She peered at me curiously and posed the question, "What brings you in, Nichole?"

I paused and tried to gather my thoughts. Why was it so hard to talk about myself? When I finally started speaking, years of suppression and tears spewed out of me, landing all over her office. It was all coming out. My scary therapist, whose name I can't even remember now, sat quietly observing this shit show.

"Well, sometimes I feel so burnt out. I feel so alone. I feel so confused about what I'm supposed to be loving about my life that I just don't want to wake up in the morning."

I held my breath, waiting for her to react or shame me. In being a therapist myself, I know shaming isn't standard practice. But being vulnerable feels scary, and that part of me awaited a worst-case scenario response. My cheeks were bright red from admitting my real thoughts out loud. I was waiting for her to wince or jot down in her notebook how crazy I was. I was even ready for her to call the psych ward and have me committed.

She didn't.

"So, you're feeling suicidal." She said it calmly, not even presenting it as a question. It was a statement offered with zero hints of panic.

"Um. No. Well, maybe. I don't know. Do you ever just feel like jerking your car off the road?" *Oh my god, I can't believe I said that.*

"It sounds like you're feeling overwhelmed."

Fucking duh. I stared her down, suddenly totally annoyed. I couldn't possibly be paying for this. This was the part where she was supposed to chime in with something brilliant that would make me shift perspectives and feel relieved for admitting to a perfect stranger that I wanted to drive my car off a bridge. I said nothing. I waited her out. She wasn't winning this one.

"You know what's interesting?" I rolled my eyes as she dove into more therapy babble, "I don't think you're depressed at all, Nichole. I think you're suppressed. You've spent your whole life playing roles for everyone to the point you don't know who you are without them. You don't know how to ask for what you want. Because you haven't even started to identify it."

Those damn tears again.

I left her office after using up a half box of Kleenex. I felt so relieved after just letting it all out in an honest, safe space that I only saw her two more times. But that was the first time I recognized the soul I had been ignoring. I felt like Julia Roberts in that 90's movie *Runaway Bride*: I didn't know how I liked my eggs. I had always just eaten what everyone else liked or wanted me to like. *I eventually came to find out I hate eggs.*

Getting open and honest about your truth is essential to your comeback. Clinical psychologist Dr. Edith Eger once explained that the opposite of depression is expression.[12] Inner truth will set you free. But what they don't tell you is sometimes the inner truth takes some practice to hear in the first place.

You can recognize the truth by how it feels. Untruth physically feels uncomfortable and foreign. Psychologists call this *discernment*. Discernment is how our soul uses our physical body to say, "Hell to the yes, I want this! This is so right for me!" or "This is absolutely not going to work." A true "yes" feels calm. It feels centered, spacious, and grounded. An energetic hug, really. It's like saying your name over and over again and knowing that it is indeed your name. But if you start calling yourself Don Juan from Tucson (unless that's your real name!), it's going to feel wrong.

Many people get a twinge in their stomach, a sinking in their heart, or a tightness in their shoulders or throat when they speak or think something that's against their inner truth.

You can practice how your soul says "yes" by saying something you love out loud on repeat, scanning your body, and feeling those feelings of lightness and love. Then practice paying attention to what your body does when it's not in alignment by saying that you hate the exact same thing you said you loved.

For example, I love hibachi. I *love* hibachi. This second, I can envision and smell the soup and the yum yum sauce. "I love hibachi." I instantly feel my heart swelling with love, excitement, and light. I feel joy from the inside. This is a "yes" for my body and soul!

Let's switch it. Take the same thing you just said you loved and now say you hate it. "I hate hibachi. It's gross. I hate hibachi. It's the worst."

I can feel my stomach twist and flip. My heart sinks, and my body feels heavier.

This might seem like a silly example—unless you deeply understand how much I love hibachi. Now it's your turn to pick something to love and see how your body responds to it. Say you love that person, place, or thing over and over. Feel what that truth feels like in your body. Notice *where* in your body you feel it. Now flip the script. Say you hate that same thing. Over and over. See where in your body your soul is telling you, "Hell no, this is not true."

The reality is your soul *never* lies, even when your head does. Your soul won't let you bullshit yourself or anyone else. It will stay steady, whispering your truth quietly until you choose differently for yourself.

Another important piece of reclaiming yourself is not just recognizing the truth in your body but finding the courage to say it out loud. Get comfortable with radical honesty. Maybe the truth of why you haven't switched jobs is that you're afraid your partner won't support you, or you're nervous about added responsibility. Maybe the reason you haven't moved out of town is that you don't want to disappoint your family by not being close by anymore. Maybe you haven't finished that book because you're scared no one will read it. *(Psst: This one's me.)*

The truth doesn't always immediately change your external world, but it does release resistance between your head and your heart, leaving room for alignment and action.

Truth doesn't require immediate action, though. Working with people over the years, I've come to realize that sometimes you don't want to acknowledge that something in your life is finished because you are terrified of what the next step looks like. You might feel that if you admit the truth, then you'll need to scramble to figure out what to do next. It's not true! You can acknowledge the truth, allowing it to guide you to the answers and inspired action. *We will talk more about our intuition later.*

One of my favorite practices for getting honest is to look at yourself in the mirror and say, "The truth is…" and see what comes up within you. You can also make that a journaling exercise. Maybe the truth is you hate your job but are scared to leave because you've been broke before and don't want to be again. Maybe the truth is you're unhappy in your relationship but have been together so long you can't imagine starting over. Maybe the truth is you'd love to dress in a way that's more authentic but are scared of what people will think.

Whatever your truth is, get to know it. Get it out of your body and into a place where you can really take a look at it. We cannot make major changes in our life without total honesty about what is working and what isn't. Remember, we don't need to know how things will get better, we just have to trust that they will. Practice discerning how your soul responds to your yeses and nos. Practice writing down or telling your truth out loud in a safe space. Expression releases depression. Honesty creates space for your life to change. The tools for exactly how will come in the next part.

Chapter 8:
WHOSE RULES ARE THEY?

My childhood summers in Upstate New York were spent in my backyard, specifically near the pool. Not *in* the pool, mind you, just near it. When the water would splash out from the typical cannonball contests, it would hit the dirt and bring to life a community of creepy, crawly insects. My favorite pastime in early elementary school was collecting the bugs, worms, and anything else greeting the surface.

I would spend my Saturdays in my favorite yellow sundress, filling a matching yellow bucket to the brim with as many creepy crawlers as I could find. The pill bugs that curled up into a ball were pure gold.

One afternoon I took my new favorite worms, Harry and Larry, over to see my best friend Jenny at her grandmother's house. Excited to show Jenny today's findings, I grabbed the worms out of my bucket and placed them on the front porch table. Jenny's grandmother yelped as if I had pinched her.

"Get those off of there!" she exclaimed. I giggled. "Proper little girls do not play with worms. We leave that to the boys."

I scooped up Harry and Larry, shoving them back into the dirt bucket, using the bottom of my sundress to wipe off the leftover dirt residue. There were lots of rules for little girls. But I suppose there were lots of rules for little boys, too.

Unspoken and spoken rules shape your mindset about what's okay and not okay. Rules aren't always as simple as the numbered outlines that get passed out on the first day of kindergarten. They are so much more than that. They might be designed by anger, disappointment, or disgust from someone you value and care about. They might be shaped by fears of not fitting in or embedded through guilt and shame of what is *supposed* to happen. We acquire rules and beliefs from everyone. Before we know it, our personalities have been shaped and conditioned by past experiences and external influences.

We can recognize if these rules have a negative impact on our life if they are stopping us from achieving our goals, keeping us from growing professionally or personally, halting us from moving forward or making progress, or ceasing us from making good choices or taking positive risks.

You may recognize these rules or limiting beliefs by where in your life you find yourself saying, "I can't because____." Beliefs are often disguised as excuses. Other limiting beliefs may show up, like, "I don't have enough time," "I'll never move forward," "I'm not good enough, smart enough, or talented enough," or "I'm too old/overweight/poor, etc." What beliefs or rules are keeping you stuck?

We can get curious about where these beliefs came from or the purpose they once served. Then, we get to challenge them. We get to ask if they are true or helpful. We get to see if there are any exceptions to them.

Questions and curiosity are how we take what we've always done, how we've always acted, and what we are "supposed" to do, say, or be and step into who we really are.

When we can say, "I've been doing this or feeling this way for years, but I don't know if it's the best way." It becomes the perfect opportunity to close our eyes, put our hands on our hearts, and ask the bigger questions, "Do I want this for me, or did someone else want this for me? Did I want this at one point in my life, but now it no longer feels right? Is this even true? Is this thought or belief helping me get to where I want to go?" I truly believe our disconnection from our truth and our soul happens without us even realizing it. When we haven't stopped long enough to ask ourselves the hard questions.

I once went through a Southern KFC drive-thru. They were out of normal biscuits, so the woman suggested cornbread instead. "Oh! No thanks, I don't really like cornbread," I said. She handed me the bag and, in the kindest Southern accent, said, "Well, I put some in there just in case. You can either eat it or throw it out the wind-er." *I threw it out the window.*

Let's think of your current rules and ways of existing as the cornbread. Perhaps it's the idea that you're not al-lowed to take alone time once you become a mother or that the only way to get ahead in your career is to work insane hours. Maybe it's the limiting belief that you can't change your career path after forty or the thought that you're not qualified for a job you really want. Explore ev-erything. Then decide to either keep it or "throw it out the winder."

This is your life. You're not trapped living by the rules of other people or the beliefs your old self had. You're the only one who gets to live it. You are the only one who deals with the emotions, feelings, and sensations within your body. You are the only one who experiences suffer-ing when shit isn't working. If the rules that were hand-ed to you are no longer working, you'll, without a doubt, know.

You'll feel it in your body. You'll feel dissatisfied or heavy emotionally. How you feel, both in your body and mind, acts as an indicator that something needs to shift. Remember earlier when we talked about telling the truth? Releasing other people's rules and expectations requires you to strengthen your inner voice. Get honest and clear, then question everything.

Coming back to yourself means examining the rules and beliefs that you have had for a long time. Become highly aware of limiting beliefs or rules that are blocking you or keeping you stuck. Try on different hats, thoughts, and habits, seeing which one feels right in this phase of your life. Question what beliefs are working and in alignment and what ones aren't true or need to be tossed out the proverbial window. Breaking the rules comes with giving yourself permission to be or do whatever it is authentically you!

You get to create the rules of your life. If you want worms on your front porch table because they bring you joy, bring on the worms. Feel into your body to see how the rule or belief makes you feel. You get to design your life and personality in a true and supportive way, not of who you've been but who you want to become. In our comeback, we make our own rules.

Chapter 9:

WHAT DO YOU EXPECT?

I'm a bad texter. And no, I'm not just someone who says that. I'm a classic terrible texter. You can confirm this with any of my closest friends. The demands from running a business on my phone often leave me with anxiety, as I feel pulled in so many directions. I often put my phone away, have it face down, or haphazardly open messages while I'm at a stop light or the school pickup line. I forget that I've even opened them by the time I get home. If I do text back, it's typically only to set up a time we will chat on the phone or meet up in person.

Now, my texting, or lack thereof, for some people, is a trigger. I've had friends who seemed angry with me for not responding or taking a full week and a half to do so. And I can definitely acknowledge my poor technological etiquette! But have you ever noticed we create expectations with others as a means to measure our worth? Just as we have rules given to us by people, we also have rules for *them* disguised as expectations.

For some people, texting back promptly and often is an immediate sign of love and respect. Their expectation: frequency and immediacy of contact are directly associated with love and appreciation. But for me, I want to see your eyes light up when you tell me a fun story you've been waiting to tell me. I want to hear your voice or watch you on FaceTime when you tell me you got the promotion. I want to be energetically present with the people I love and care about, which is much harder to do over text.

We've consciously and unconsciously developed rules for other people that they do not know exist. Imagine playing Candyland with someone who is operating under a totally different set of rules. They skip straight from start to gumdrop pass. When people play by different rules than we do, we are forced to question if they are cheating or if it's us who don't know how to play.

When people do not follow the rules we have set in our heads, we decide what it means. That meaning is usually a judgment toward them or validation of our own insecurities, giving us examples and justification that we aren't loved and cared about.

Interacting with other humans is kind of a shit show. We all have different rules, values, and upbringings dictating how we believe relationships and life should go. We have a full list of what to do and what *not* to do unconsciously embedded into us. This is why we might feel defeated and unseen when someone tells us they love us by fixing our car instead of giving compliments or sending flowers.

Remember, as we are exploring our expectations: other people aren't the same as you. That's what makes the world an incredible place to be. If you're expecting a guest to volunteer to help clean up after your dinner party because that's what *you'd* do, you're setting yourself up for disappointment. Our secret rules for other people can set the stage for anger and resentment. Don't get me wrong—we can definitely be selective about who we let in our lives, and we can set standards. But we also need to understand our expectations and how to communicate what we need or want from the people around us.

I'm a really vulnerable person. *Obvi.* I find it easy to share what's in my head and heart with people close to me. And because I'm a therapist, I have a lot of people sharing their innermost secrets with me.

This has really messed me up in my personal relationships! I expect the same therapeutic level of openness from people I meet and have as friends. This screws with how I perceive other people because some people naturally take longer to open up. Some people see me as an acquaintance rather than a safe repository for every deep thought and heart wound.

In the past, I've felt hurt by this or not valued because I want everyone to trust me that much. But I've learned to accept it's not only okay but normal that they don't.

Being clear in our communication directs people to know how to care for us. "I love and appreciate it when you help me fold laundry. It's important to me that we do this together more often. Can you help me again tomorrow night?" or "I love having you around, but when you talk poorly about other people, I feel uncomfortable. Can we keep our conversations focused on something else?"

The easiest way to take an unmet expectation to a fulfilled desire is by recognizing and getting very clear on what we need from others and for ourselves and then sharing it. After all, we are all out here wanting to be seen, heard, and loved. *Expression, not suppression.*

When we are trying to feel heard, we often use "you" statements to communicate, most commonly, only when we reach our breaking point. Yelling, "You never help me around the house!" "You" statements immediately put the other person in a defensive position. In an Ed Mylett Podcast interview with relationship expert John Kim, Kim discussed how when you get defensive in an argument, your prefrontal cortex, which is your brain's area of reasoning, shuts down, making you, or your partner, literally unreasonable.[13] He suggests trying to understand before trying to be understood.

A better way of sharing a need without creating defensiveness is by creating "I" statements. "I" statements look like "I feel ____ when this need isn't met. What helps me feel better is when (insert action here) happens." For example, "I feel alone when I feel like I am the only one helping around the house. What makes me feel loved, valued, and respected is when you help me without being asked." "I" statements help you speak from your own experience rather than accusing.

Now that we've clarified what our expectations are and communicated how we feel loved, seen, or heard. We may notice a few things. We may notice that we've found common ground, understanding, and resolution with the people we love. We also might see that some people are unwilling to treat us in a way that feels good, no matter how clear we are. This is where our next chapter on boundaries comes into play.

Understanding your expectations for others is necessary for positive experiences with people we love. Get clear on what makes you feel loved, seen, and heard so you can communicate it. Be mindful that your secret expectations aren't leading to resentment or insecurity. Communicate your needs by using "I" statements and refrain from using "you" statements. From here, we get to make choices about who gets to stay in our lives and who doesn't. We can learn to set boundaries accordingly.

Chapter 10:

BOUNDARY SETTER

When my sister was sixteen, she met a guy named James. At the time, James was an interesting, live-life-on-the-edge kind of guy. James lived in a rough part of town and often told stories about getting in fights with different groups in the area. I was fourteen when they met. I remember sitting in his living room with his pet snake wrapped around my hand and passing around a bottle of peppermint schnapps and a joint while he talked about how his buddy had been arrested because of last night's knife fight.

For a while, the thrill of the bad-boy lifestyle enthralled both my sister and me. I still had braces but always tried to match my energy to keep up with the cool *Dangerous Minds* lifestyle James and his friends led.

The more frequently James and his buddies ended up in jail, the more I distanced myself from the group. My sister didn't. This teenage relationship eventually morphed into a dangerous, domestically violent relationship. James' drinking and drug use would escalate over the years, leading to verbal, emotional, and eventually, extreme physical abuse where my sister would end up in the hospital.

I don't share this story often because her journey isn't mine to tell. But what I can share is the way that it impacted me. When you're watching someone you love and care about lose their light to toxic relationships or addiction, it can be easy to want to save them. Remember the people-pleasing tendencies I discussed before? They went into full force with her.

On numerous occasions, my father and I would get calls in the middle of the night from my sister or police officers asking us to go get her from a domestic dispute. I slept with my phone volume on high, fearful of the day when he would take it too far. I was always on edge, not knowing if she was safe or if this was the time he would kill her.

At one point, she moved in with me, my husband, and my two-year-old. She reformed for a while, made some strides, and got a new job. But eventually, she went back to James. It broke my heart every time. I found myself in survival mode about a relationship that wasn't even mine.

The last time I helped her was after she had her daughter. James took a swing at her while she was holding the baby. I dropped everything, canceled clients, and drove her to Florida so she could be safe with my mother. She drove herself back to be with James about two weeks later.

My husband and I agreed that this is where we needed to draw the line. We were drained and exhausted and recognized we could not help someone who was unwilling to help themselves.

Setting boundaries when you are worried about someone's safety or health is challenging but important. Everyone will have opinions about what the right move is. There are people who will say, "C'mon, it's your sister," or "You have to sacrifice everything for your family." I'm here to state the potentially unpopular opinion that if another person's life choices are taking everything out of you and draining your mental health, well-being, or finances, you don't.

This is an extreme example. Not all boundaries will be as obvious or intense. Establishing healthy boundaries in your life is the key to both maintaining your sanity and strengthening your identity. Boundaries are guidelines and limits put into place to let others know what ways of behaving are okay or not okay. Boundaries are a way of saying, "I'm willing or unwilling to have this be part of my life." Poor personal boundaries lead to resentment, anger, or burnout, according to Nelson's 2016 study.[14]

Setting the boundary first comes with getting clear on what's not working. From here, you can set up the boundary by being direct and clear in your communication. You do not need to apologize or over-explain your boundary. Some examples of setting a healthy boundary include "If you say that to my child again, you won't be able to directly text them anymore." or "Please text me and wait for a response before stopping by."

In more intense scenarios, like with my sister, you can establish your love in the boundary by saying, "I love you, but trying to save you is hurting my family and me. Next time you're in trouble, here's a list of some shelters or advocates that will be helpful to you."

Important to note is that the person with whom you are setting the boundary may not like your boundary. Many people who are manipulative, controlling, used to taking advantage of you, or abusive do not handle boundaries being set. You may need to, temporarily or permanently, cut these people off. The good news is a person's poor response to your boundary doesn't mean you shouldn't have set it. Your job isn't to be responsible for their response, but only for setting the boundary with love and respect, then sticking to it.

You may feel guilty or selfish, especially if you've spent years people-pleasing or abandoning yourself. Al-anon has a great phrase called "detaching with compassion." Setting a boundary also doesn't mean you don't love and care about that person. It does, however, mean you're not willing to take responsibility for their emotional immaturity or poor choices and that you have the right to care about and prioritize yourself and your well-being.

Boundaries take practice to get used to. You may even start with smaller, subtler boundaries like telling the masseuse the pressure is too hard or correcting a mixed-up order at a restaurant. Smaller boundaries help you build confidence to set larger boundaries. While setting boundaries, it's important to remember your feelings and needs are not just valid, but important. <u>You are responsible for what you allow in your life.</u> Sacrificing what you need or stuffing down your real feelings only hurts you.

Start by paying close attention to if a situation or person is depleting you or making you feel bad. Get clear about what isn't working or how it is impacting you. From here, you can shift into communicating a boundary. Remember, you're not responsible for their response. It may be helpful to practice setting smaller boundaries before diving into bigger boundaries.

Chapter 11:

THE PEOPLE AROUND YOU

When I was in high school, I dated a guy who would get me to leave a party by picking fights with me. We would be having a great time, and then suddenly, his energy would shift. He would say mean things, and I would get upset and leave. Later, I found out he would do this because his *other* girlfriend was on her way. The one he had had for three years, whom everyone knew existed but me. *To be fair, we went to different schools, and this was pre-social media!*

High school was semi-tragic for me and my self-esteem in a lot of ways. This was mainly because I chose a series of toxic relationships, which negatively impacted how I viewed myself. I'd find myself with people who didn't think too highly of themselves or couldn't accept responsibility for their actions, so I easily absorbed the blame.

I could take an entire book to talk about healthy vs. unhealthy relationships. *We don't have that kind of time!* However, I truly believe that you become what you are most consistently around, so we have to chat this out for a bit.

Think about it for a minute; if you are with people who find their fun by getting wasted every night, it would be hard to be a person who doesn't drink. If you are friends with a group of people who hold certain bold political opinions, it might be hard to hold an opposing viewpoint. This isn't just true for behavior and beliefs but for your mood too! It's hard to be happy around a group that's always angry or be extremely wealthy in a group that complains about not having enough money. We match energies as much as we match beliefs. So, it's time to talk about who's on your team and who, well, isn't.

When we are talking about relationships, I want you to consider that they don't have to be romantic in nature. A relationship constitutes friends, family, or anyone from whom you desire connection, love, or approval. Pay attention to how *you* act in a relationship. Closely note if you find yourself misaligning with what you want or believe solely to please someone or fit in. Create awareness if you're hiding parts of yourself to make sure they always approve. Do you catch yourself shrinking in order to not become "too much"?

Paying attention to the influence your immediate circle has on you is vital to make your comeback. Are you more yourself or less yourself with them? Is it safe to be yourself around them? Do you have to shrink to make them like you? Do you have to overperform or overachieve to feel relevant or noticed?

What and whom we let into our mind and energy is critical. The people around us help design our inner dialogue and sense of self. When it comes to our life, our soul is in dire need of cheerleaders. People who know our potential. Friends who refuse to let us be anything less than our stellar, most awesome selves. People who love and accept our faults but will also encourage us to work towards our best selves when we've gotten sidetracked.

You'll know your real cheerleaders because they'll show up whether you win or lose the game. They show up, and you don't have to ask them to.

It's hard enough to believe in yourself in a world that flashes its achievements more intensely than a college jock at a frat party. Who in your life makes you feel like a million bucks? Who in your life can support you without trying to sway your direction? Who in your life loves you even when you're being shitty? *Because sometimes we're shitty.* Who is someone who sees your potential and challenges you with love and care?

In the book *Attached* by Amir Levine, the author explains that when we feel authentic and secure in our relationships, we can reach our full potential more quickly and easily.[15] When we do not feel secure in our relationships, we often become distracted by the problems in the relationship and fail to reach for more.

We are wired for connection, but our deepest, truest connections come from being exactly ourselves. We achieve more when we are loved, supported, and properly held accountable. Not to say you can't kick ass with crappy people around you. Some people do better and aim higher because they've been doubted. But I'm a firm believer you are deeply influenced by what you surround yourself with.

Our job in our comeback is to scan our social circle and take an honest look at the way it impacts us. Is it helping you grow or keeping you stuck? Are you supported and honored for who you are? Who can you be most yourself around? The key in the observation is to consider what type of people will help us grow into our best selves. We must be willing to distance ourselves from the wrong people. We must intentionally search for people who are more aligned with where are going rather than who we have been.

Chapter 12:

BRITNEY SAID IT'S TOXIC

As I mentioned with the example of my sister, toxic relationships can wreak havoc on every area of our lives. We can get so glued to one person, place, or thing we believe is keeping us afloat that we sacrifice our health, mental health, goals, dreams, and other positive relationships.

You don't need to have a crappy romantic relationship to be in a toxic situation. This can be a living situation, a court case, a job, or any situation that gives you both mental obsession and distinct emotional highs and lows. Some red flags for unhealthy or toxic relationships include lack of support, conversations filled with criticism, feeling like you can't trust the other person, patterns of disrespect for either you or your time, feeling like your needs are ignored, not openly being able share your needs or desires, walking on eggshells or feeling like you have to be careful of what you say, feeling like you give significantly more than you receive, feeling like you can't be yourself, and feeling drained from the relationship.

When our body gets used to being treated poorly by anything or anyone, that low emotion becomes our baseline emotion. A baseline emotion is the feeling we are most commonly in. That's the emotion our brain will try to encourage us back to whenever we veer off.

In terms of a toxic situation or relationship, when you typically have a slew of negative experiences followed by one positive moment, whether that's recognition from a toxic boss or a good deed from a toxic lover, it elevates your emotional state from that baseline of negativity. We immediately link the good feeling to the situation or person, creating a *trauma bond*. You now associate your positive feelings with this toxic person or situation.

In the most extreme cases, we see this as Stockholm Syndrome. Think of when a kidnapping victim falls in love with their kidnapper. Imagine being starving and trapped in someone's basement. *I don't know why I always think of a basement, but…basement.* Think of being at your lowest, your hungriest, your basic needs not being met—and then someone offers you a Snickers bar. We can get sparked when we are low by the smallest acts of kindness, even from someone who's consistently been treating us poorly.

Our brain becomes focused and hopeful when there's inconsistency in rewards. You don't have to be kidnapped to experience a bonding or addiction to something bad for you, though. You just need to be in an emotionally charged situation that is inconsistent in its rewards.

American behavioral psychologist B.F. Skinner called this type of interaction intermittent reinforcement conditioning.[16] When we are rewarded inconsistently, our brain gets addicted to the potential of the reward. However, if we stop and look around at what the day-to-day experience is, we may not feel that same high. This is why we can't always trust our feelings when it comes to toxic relationships. We have the potential to bond to the wrong things: things that hurt us, keep us stuck, or aren't the healthiest option for us.

Toxic relationships are the rare situation in which I will note that your interpretation of your intuition may be off. As YouTuber Anna Runkle, The Crappy Childhood Fairy points out, when we are in unhealthy dynamics, we try to crap-fit our intuition, meaning we try to make our intuitive feelings into something we want them to be rather than hearing your intuitive nudges for what they really are. Deep down, I believe we always know the truth when something isn't healthy for us, even when we deeply desire it or feel addicted to it.

If you feel like you may be in a toxic relationship, I want you to really look at a couple things. How much time do you spend thinking about or focusing on them? Many times, toxic relationships pull us outside ourselves, meaning we pay less attention to taking care of ourselves and focusing on our own dreams or goals and instead spend our time worrying about how that person feels and what they are doing. How do you feel most of the time? If you are in a situation that feels defeating, dangerous, or bad more frequently than good, you are likely mistaking fear and attachment wounding for intuition or "soulmate love."

As much as I love the idea of soulmates or twin flames and genuinely believe there are people we are meant to interact with, these ideologies have many people staying in unhealthy relationships that diminish their light and distract from their potential. Please don't accept less from people in your life because you've been told they are your soulmate.

When we recognize that we have a toxic relationship in our life, we get to decide what we do from here. As I said, toxic situations can feel addictive, but we have the power to step out of them and move forward in our lives. Part of our work is redirecting our energy and focus. Remember how we talked about the seagulls? If we feed a seagull, more will come. When we start to redirect our focus back to ourselves, our goals, and our dreams, we begin to take our power back. This means we have to come back to ourselves and redirect our focus back to our internal space. This may mean turning your phone off and finding a creative outlet. Prioritizing healthy friendships. Pouring the energy into a fun, fulfilling hobby like exercising, writing, or volunteering.

Another important piece will be when you're ready to truly step into your power, cutting off communication. This may first look like quitting a job that is toxic or blocking your ex. Even if you're not ready to block them, you can put their contact on mute for the day, put your phone away for the day, or set a verbal boundary that you need space for the week. Work with your own willingness. Take it one day at a time. Remember, the more you focus on this dynamic, the more you'll strengthen your focus on it. Keep bringing your focus back to yourself and building trust in yourself. Ask yourself what you truly want, not what you're willing to settle for.

Now it's time to take inventory. Who's on your team? Whose voice needs drowning out? Pay attention to your body and energy levels before and after you've been with people. Is anyone giving you inconsistent rewards? Who leaves you feeling inspired? Who leaves you feeling exhausted? Bring your focus back to yourself and your growth. The rest of the tips in this book will help you reprogram your mind to detach from unhealthy situations. *Hang in there and keep reading. I got you.*

Toxic Relationship Checklist

- Feeling Drained/walking on eggshells
- Feeling like you can't be yourself
- Lack of Trust/ Dishonesty
- All take, no give
- Unreliability or constant judgment
- Persistent unhappiness associated with the relationship
- Hiding how you really feel

PART 3.

THE PART WHERE YOU UNDO

Sometimes the shift back into your power is something you have to wait for. It's a readiness. A certain feeling. *You'll totally know.* Even picking up this book might have been a nudge in the right direction—your soul calling you to level up.

We can try to force change all we wish. We can say we're over it or make bold moves and enforce New Year's resolutions, but true change must involve your mind, actions, and soul being in alignment. Sometimes our soul knows what we need to do way before our head connects the dots and fear moves out of the way.

In order to truly undo it, we have to get honest and clear on what isn't working and why. Now that we have that clarity, we can dive not just into knowing life can be better but into the practices to make it that way.

The Part Where You Undo promises to take the awareness of what isn't working and give you actionable tools to begin to make changes in your mind, habits, and life. I promise you don't just have to wish to be a better, more healed version of yourself. I will guide you through powerful practices that not only worked for my clients but also for me in my darkest times. I know if you put them into practice, they will work for you, too!

Chapter 13:

MAKING THE COMMITMENT

Although I shared this in my first book, I'm going to say loudly for the people in the back because, well, it's my favorite quote by Jen Sincero: "It's not your fault if you're fucked up. It's your fault if you stay fucked up." Work through your shit. Process your emotions. Hold space. Cry it out. Realize the patterns of behaviors and thoughts as well as the roles you've played. And then commit to being better. The future you is so excited for you to step back into your power.

I'm a therapist both by degree (three, to be exact) and nature. I've held space for some really tough stuff. I know life can come at you, throw you curveballs, and cause serious wounding. While it's helpful and important to understand why you are the way you are and to hold compassion for what you've gone through, it can be dangerous to get stuck there and play victim to it.

I've had so many people in my office saying things like, "Well, I pushed them away because my dad left when I was a kid." It's fantastic to know you have a reaction based on a past event. We can hold compassion and sympathy for that little kid who was abandoned by someone they deeply loved. We can also appreciate your body and mind's way of trying to protect you when that occurred. We can even explore the ways that you're triggered in the present day, hold compassion, and get any needed therapy.

But the next part of that process is deciding not to give it power anymore, which involves shifting your focus to designing your future. How are you going to emotionally regulate yourself to make a new choice the next time a triggering experience arises? How are you going to vocalize your thoughts clearly to get your needs met or to set a boundary?

When we stay in victim mode too long, we lose access to our power. We hand over our power to that terrible thing, person, or situation, letting it be bigger than us. We can potentially become victims of our triggers and feel like we have no control over ourselves or our minds. This also can give us an excuse to avoid the responsibility of making changes and progress in our lives.

Maybe other people weren't able to give you what you wanted or needed in the past, but we aren't in the past anymore. We're here, in the now. And now you get to give yourself everything you deserve and everything you once needed.

Don't you dare say to me, "This is just how I am because this happened to me." Yes, events change you and shape you, but you still get to have an epic life if *you* decide to! Choice is everything. Choice is where you regain your power.

Right now, you have to commit to yourself and the up-leveled version of you waiting to emerge. You're worthy of more. You deserve so much love and connection. You're worthy of love and belonging. You're worth more than that situation had to offer you. You have everything you need to move forward. It's time to take responsibility for your life right now. It's time to fight for your future. Choose better.

Chapter 14:

SURVIVAL VS. INTENTION

At one point in time, my two kids were obsessed with the block-building video game Minecraft. Like, they spent their own money to go to a Minecraft Convention. I've never been a big video game person, but when the kids ask me to play, I try not to say no.

I played with my older daughter, Camryn, that first time. Cam and I spent time constructing a mansion on a hill overlooking a waterfall. We collected watermelons, dug for materials, and named our pet sheep. She showed me all of the cool spots she had constructed in her world, including a massive library.

The second time I played Minecraft was with my youngest, Kylie. As we were building, the background changed to night. She said we needed to hide in the house we had just made. Zombies and creepers began to emerge, trying to break in. I was so confused. What I knew of Minecraft is that there wasn't anything trying to kill you—you just made cool stuff! What I didn't know is Kylie had switched us from *creative* mode to *survival* mode, which she found hilarious. In survival mode, you build to stay alive, not just for fun. She laughed her butt off watching me fight off creepers, not even knowing what button to press to defend myself. I remember asking her, "Kylie, why would we choose survival mode, if we can choose creative mode instead?" She giggled, explaining it was funny to mess with me.

Then I was thinking, do we do this in our world? Do we choose a reactive, survival mode when we could choose the creative one? In survival mode, we are stuck reacting and responding to our world (aka stressing the heck out), whereas in creative mode, we are intentionally building our life and trusting the Universe to show up for us.

Prehistorically, when our bodies and minds went into survival mode, it meant there was a danger or threat at the door. A wooly mammoth was stampeding toward us or another tribe was coming to take over our village. Our bodies would need the adrenaline rush and the extra blood pumping in order to fight or quickly flee the situation.

This makes sense if you're a caveman. But you're not a caveman, and you don't need this survival feature to activate in everyday situations. This will leave you in a perpetual state of stress induced by your perception alone.

For example, let's say your boyfriend or girlfriend consistently calls you at noon. It is now 1 p.m. and you have not heard from them. *Gasp*. What if they died in a car wreck and were dead on the side of the road? What if they are cheating on you or no longer interested in you? The story your brain creates will be dependent on your personal fear narrative. Your heart starts racing from this perceived mind event. Your adrenals activate. This forces your brain to look for options of relief—anything to relieve the very real panic of feeling like you're in danger.

I can't stress enough that this event *isn't real.* You made meaning out of your partner not calling at the right time, igniting a full-body stress response. Our brain has no idea what is real and what is made up. It will activate the same energy and emotions for a perceived event as a real one. We can use this to our advantage or let it rule us to our detriment. Come to find out, despite your freak-out, your partner was not dead in a ditch, just pulled into a meeting.

When the brain shifts into survival mode, it stops using its creative power. In that setting, the brain becomes consumed with combating danger. It's almost impossible to hear your intuition in survival mode. The rush of stress hormones looks to fight, freeze, or flight, forcing your brain to only access the limited information directly in front of you—what's necessary to stay alive. In a truly threatening scenario, looking for an exit or preparing to fight would be appropriate. However, on a day-to-day basis, survival mode can leave you feeling stuck, exhausted, and like you have no other options.

When we are in this high-stress survival mode for prolonged periods of time, we forget that we are a creative force. We're also exhausted. It takes an immense amount of internal and physiological resources to be re-active, fearful, or anxious. Even our cavemen ancestors weren't just fighting at all times. Gorgeous paintings and scripted stories can be found carved into walls of caves. They invented and designed and found new ways to en-sure their kids' future.

Some people stay in an energy of chaos long after a negative event. They keep themselves stuck in a state of stress by envisioning the bad thing over and over or talking about their worry with anyone who will listen. Remember that the more we revisit an experience, the more our brain thinks it is happening now. We can get addicted to being in a state of stress, and it becomes our baseline emotion. Feeling stuck or stressed is a sure-fire sign you've forgotten you have the power to switch modes.

You can take a moment in a state of stress and ask yourself, "Which mode am I choosing? What am I en-visioning happening? How is this impacting my body and mood?" I'll always encourage you to step back into your power and create your world. Why choose to worry about zombies and hide away, terrified that you're going to lose all your gold if you could just switch modes and create a beautiful mansion on the hillside overlooking a waterfall?

This isn't Minecraft, but this *is* your life. You can choose to stay in a limited, stressful mode, or shift into a loving, trusting, creative mode the minute you realize that option is there. *Hint: it's always been there.*

Intentional, creative living is simply a mental choice, a decision. This may look like creating awareness when your brain starts to go in a negative spiral. It might be catching yourself when you are catastrophizing, envisioning the worst-case scenario. Don't underestimate the power of breathing slowly in and slowly out to de-escalate your energy and stress. We can slow everything down, including our thoughts, when we take a moment to just focus on our breath.

You might want to find a neutralizing activity, like going for a walk. You could use an affirmation like, "I trust the Universe is always working in my favor." You can just take a deep breath and focus on the flow of air down through your lungs and back out. This brings your energy and attention to the present moment. Making this intentional choice when you feel stressed out or overwhelmed is the first step in taking your power back.

A quick way to regulate your nervous system and switch out of survival mode is to bring your attention and focus back to your physical body. This could mean squeezing your muscles, holding them tight, and then relaxing them. Another way to bring your energy back into your control and back to your body is to play the senses game. Start by naming five things you see, four things you hear, three things you feel, two things you smell, and one thing you taste. You can even use your physical senses to calm panic by holding ice cubes or sucking on a lemon or Sour Patch Kids. These tactics pull the brain's attention back to a grounded place to make a different choice while helping to calm and regulate your nervous system.

Intentional living means deciding what is directly in front of you isn't all there is. Recognize that your brain doesn't have all the known routes to get what you want, but your soul and Universe do. A black hole moment does not need to become a black hole life.

Survival is your body's way of saying "We're going to look for the obvious and do what we've always done." But how boring is that? It's a total denial of your power as a co-creator of this magnificent Universe. Especially when we want to be working toward creating a new and better future, we can't afford to stay in mental patterns that recreate the past and won't let us move on. The Universe is abundant in options for bettering your life. Your job is to just recognize what mode you're in. If you need a little help, don't forget to use your physical senses to regulate your nervous response shifting back into your power and out of survival mode.

Chapter 15:

SCARCITY OR POSSIBILITY

I finished my bachelor's degree when my daughter was a year old. If you've ever survived the first year of having a child, you'll understand somehow pulling a 4.0 GPA and taking my finals four days after delivering her was nothing short of miraculous. *I still have no idea how I did it.*

When it came to applying for graduate school to become a counselor, I was excited and nervous. Having a child so young and having no help watching her meant that any time I wasn't with her, I had to pay someone to be with her. Our financial turmoil was growing as it was. I realized I couldn't afford to do the extra volunteer work required on every single grad school application.

Rejection letter after rejection letter made its way into my hands, clearly indicating that although my grades were impressive, they were also looking for someone who was well-rounded in their extracurriculars and volunteer work.

I couldn't compete with it. I was heartbroken. I had done all I could do to survive school, the lack of sleep, having a child at twenty years old, and my husband working twelve-hour days to supplement our income from my being in school. My life circumstances were blocking the future I had envisioned for myself. There appeared to be no way forward.

I very distinctly remember a conversation with a friend of mine at the time. I told her it was looking like grad school wouldn't be an option for me. She looked at me and said, "Nichole, there are like a million colleges with counseling programs. Have you applied to all of them? No? Then how can you say that?"

She had a valid point. How badly did I want this? Was I willing to apply to schools out of the area? I was so caught up in the rejections I shut down instead of persisting. I had created limiting beliefs. I couldn't do *this* because of *that*. I couldn't get into grad school because I had a kid too young. I had created an all-or-nothing mentality. Just because some schools had rejected me, I had told myself that they all would. That they would all require evidence of something I couldn't produce.

Now, let me just say, rejection is hard AF. I'm not going to downplay the fact that it hurts to know that someone, something, or a situation you were really, really excited about isn't the right one for you. But keep in mind: nothing truly meant for you rejects you.

All-or-nothing thinking in rejection situations is dangerous. Deciding that one or two examples represent all possibilities is destructive. The past says nothing about what you can have in your future. If you begin to decide that a breakup doesn't just mean one person has left your life but instead that you'll never find love again or that getting fired from a job doesn't just mean you need to find a new one, it means you'll be jobless and broke forever, you're setting yourself up to see only that.

All-or-nothing thinking comes from a scarcity mindset. You begin to believe the world isn't an abundant place and that there's not enough to go around. A scarcity mindset is a limiting mindset, but the Universe is expansive. A scarcity mindset breeds fear and detaches us from hope. It suggests life can't get better for you. But if you've lived long enough, you know this isn't true.

Someone once told me that believing you can't do or have something is like planning a trip and then not getting on the plane. Just because you're in New York and you want to be in South Carolina doesn't mean there aren't ways to get to South Carolina. It just means you're not there yet because you haven't found the right action to take. Just because you don't have your dream job or dream partner doesn't mean you can't have it. It just means you haven't found the right pathway to it. To summarize: Just because you're here and not there doesn't mean there isn't a pathway to get there from here.

I remember when I was first planning to move to South Carolina. It was a big freaking deal. I didn't want to buy a house because I really wanted to make sure that I liked where I was living prior to committing. *And I had never lived in a different state before!*

I looked for apartment after apartment, rental house after rental house. A few options piqued my interest, but they wouldn't accept my pets. Some would allow two pets, not three. I considered hiding my one very fat, shy cat and just not telling them. Hopelessness sank in. Perhaps this was a sign from the Universe that I wasn't supposed to move.

After a ton of searching, I locked in what I thought was the perfect fit for my family; the realtor informed me that although it hadn't been listed in the description, they were not allowing dogs. I slammed my computer shut. This was a lost cause. I wasn't going to find what I was looking for. My New York house was already up for sale. I had already announced this move publicly. And now I had nowhere to go. *Insert temper tantrum here.*

My pity party led me to a fork and an ice cream cake. But then I remembered it could be easier than I was making it. The options were not scarce, they were abundant. I felt the nudge of my intuition to take a deep breath and open the computer back up. Instead of sinking into hopelessness, I decided to focus on what it was I really wanted. I envisioned it: a three-bedroom rental that allowed pets. I wasn't asking for a cabana boy or a live-in maid. I wasn't asking for a master bedroom facing the east. Certainly, I wasn't trying to build a home on Jupiter. I just simply desired a three-bedroom apartment where my sweet shar pei and two kitties could also live.

I kept reminding myself of what I wanted and allowed myself to believe something perfect could pop up. Within thirty minutes of my original meltdown, my family and I found the perfect townhouse. We would end up living there for the next year until we built our dream home.

We never stepped foot into our townhouse prior to moving in, and luckily it ended up being bigger and better than I anticipated. It was only a fifteen-minute drive to the city of Charlotte, North Carolina. There was a brand-new kitchen and a walking trail around a small lake where we would go feed the ducks and swans nightly. *Yes, swans!*

You see, the possibility always exists. The world is abundant. There are more than enough school programs, houses, lovers, jobs, and opportunities out there. But when we are in a scarcity mindset or survival mode, we forget this. We falsely begin to believe whatever is in front of us at this very second is all there is. Whatever is rejecting us or refusing us is our only option for happiness. Our error lies in falsely believing that the world isn't a wildly abundant place.

The truth is new opportunities open up every minute for you to have the life you've been wanting. Maybe the reality already exists, but you've been so focused on what you've lost that you're unable to see more options directly in front of you. You are not an exception. The Universe doesn't shut down because you're approaching it. When you catch yourself feeling like you can't have what you want, remind yourself that the world is abundant. Be open, clear, and willing to see the next right action step to take.

Chapter 16:

UP UNTIL NOW

My Google search history is embarrassing. It consists of "Is Iceland technically Europe?" and "Who, *like* Tony Danza, died?" *If you're wondering, it's John Ritter.* Google is faithful in delivering to me exactly what I'm asking for even if I'm not really sure what I'm asking. The search engine has such a cool way of filtering billions of bits of information to show me my requests within a second of typing them in.

What if I told you that we have a Google search filter set up in our brains? Because we do! When you input a thought, your brain is engineered to look for evidence of that thought in your environment, memories, and day-to-day experiences.

To provide a basic summary, if you think shitty thoughts, your brain will look for examples that the shitty things you're thinking are true. If you think healthy thoughts or thoughts of possibility, your brain will begin to look for examples that those are true. That's it. How basic and simple our little brains can be! *I know I'm over-simplifying the incredible field of neuroscience.*

Your brain pathways find a familiar route and stick with it. It's like a software program that begins to run automatically after a while.

I won't bullshit you—acquiring new beliefs takes intention and repetition. You have to commit daily to building new beliefs and ideas. Without intentionally introducing better thoughts, your brain will return to its baseline emotion and the same thoughts it has been programmed to, no matter if that's a positive or negative experience. A 2020 study found that a person has over six thousand thoughts per day; most are repetitive from the day before.[17]

If we are programmed to think the same thoughts, we are also likely to see the same things. The same evidence. Experiencing the same conditions on repeat. No wonder life sometimes feels stale. Thinking the same thoughts is like chewing the same gum from the day before. The flavor gets lost.

The good news is your current thought process is nothing more than a culmination of your *past* thoughts and feelings. This is one of the ways our brain practices homeostasis. Without awareness or intention, your brain and thoughts will travel their most familiar route, returning you to your most commonly experienced thoughts and beliefs.

In therapist Britt Frank's book, *The Science of Stuck,* she shares that our brains aren't built for happiness; they are built for survival.[18] Being built for survival means your brain thrives by conserving energy. Similar thoughts take less energy. So, creating new beliefs takes a little work!

How do we get from Point A of a deeply depressed baseline to Point B of a fulfilled, content lifestyle? We dive in headfirst. *Literally.*

In order to see new things in our world, we have to practice thinking new thoughts or submerging ourselves in new experiences. Author and spiritual channel Abraham Hicks emphasizes that beliefs are only thoughts that we *keep* thinking.

What are you typing into your mind's Google search bar for each part of your life? Are you asking the search bar to look for examples of ways you're sick? *I mean, half the world is right now.* Are you anticipating distrust in relationships? Are you expecting high stress in your job?

These repeated thoughts create our beliefs and also act as filters for what we see in the world. For example, if you believe you're not good enough, your brain is going to look at your memories and search for matching criteria, like the time you didn't make the volleyball team or the time your co-worker was chosen for promotion over you. You're going to unconsciously search for proof in your day-to-day environment of failures or inadequacies, like fixating on a comment you made in a meeting that felt dumb.

The important part of knowing how the brain works is that it isn't that we don't also have moments of brilliance or great ideas; it's that our "not good enough" story will block or diminish them or pass them off as a lucky break, an outlier, or anomaly. Remember, our brain is only looking for proof to match our story. So, we have to be extremely careful about what story we are writing.

According to Pam Grout's book *E Squared*, the brain has billions of bits of stimuli and information coming in every given second.[19] From there, we also know that in order to prioritize what we pay attention to, our brain has to decide what information is relevant. It does this based on your beliefs.

Our perceptual filters (beliefs) are the brain's design template for what you see in your world. Perhaps you remember the time you got a new car and then suddenly started seeing this car everywhere. There wasn't some overnight overproduction of your new vehicle. Your brain just now recognizes this vehicle as important and has a filter to help it stand out.

One of my favorite tools for changing your life is something I like to call a personal inventory. *I made one for you at the end of this section!* A personal inventory is where you jot down all the categories of your life, including, but not limited to, your self-perception, relationships, career, spiritual, physical, health, and wealth. Then you explore your beliefs within them.

How are each of these areas going? Are you feeling great in your career? Is your love life a shit show? Spend an evening examining it. Write it all down. What do you believe to be true about each area? Based on that belief, knowing we see what we believe, what are you most likely going to see in your world? What would you need to change or believe differently in order to see something new?

What kind of person do you want to be? What are your personal desires or goals for each life category? See what you believe or expect in each category. Does this thought or belief work for you? What are you destined to see or experience because of this belief? What would you rather see or experience? What would you have to begin to believe to see something better?

Make it a game. When we make it fun by simply observing what we are thinking, we can laugh off the stupid thoughts that aren't helping. From there, we can start scripting our future by considering all the possibilities, especially what we would prefer. This means we can choose to regularly visit a little bit of a better thought to help create better filters.

Another cheat code to rewire your brain if you're not sure where to start is to be intentional about engaging in play or trying something new. According to the episode "Using Play to Rewire & Improve Your Brain" by The Huberman Lab Podcast, studies on play have shown that low-stakes play or being a beginner at anything increases neuroplasticity.[20] Increasing neuroplasticity is just a fancy way of saying that play, or putting yourself in new situations, allows your brain to change and form new thoughts more easily. Give yourself a chance to suck at something. Take a hip-hop fitness class, try aerial silks, or go to an event or location where you don't know other people. Push yourself out of your normal routine.

You see, your power in changing your life lies in intentionally choosing something new. Right now, you have every possibility at your fingertips. At this very moment, your current reality is nothing but a manifestation of what you believed, thought, and did in the past. You get to create a new future by starting to think, act, and choose differently now.

I remember feeling both terrified and empowered the first time I considered that my thoughts were creating my reality. I remember thinking, "Well, shit, if I'm the creator of my own experience, what I've designed thus far has kind of sucked." The good news is that from here on out, you can always become more intentional about how you live your life, what you think, and what choices you make for yourself. Start with paying attention to your thoughts. Use the personal inventory to explore what you will see in your environment based on those thoughts. Choose wisely.

Personal Inventory Worksheet pt. 1

This inventory is intended for you to look at how each area of your life is going and how your beliefs are helping our hurting you.

	HOW IT IS GOING?	WHAT DO I BELIEVE?	BASED ON MY BELIEFS, WHAT AM I LIKELY TO SEE?
My Relationship with myself			
My Romantic Relationships			
My Career/Work Life			
Finances			
My Home Life			
My Energy Level			
My Spiritual Life			
Adventures and Fun			
My Physical Body and Health			
Friendships and Social Time			

Personal Inventory Worksheet pt. 2

This part of the inventory is to look at what you'd like to change and what you'd need to begin to believe to see it!

	HOW WOULD I PREFER IT TO GO?	WHAT DO I NEED TO BELIEVE TO SEE IT?	WHAT BELIEFS AM I WILING TO TRY ON TO HELP ME GET THERE?
My Relationship with myself			
My Romantic Relationships			
My Career/Work Life			
Finances			
My Home Life			
My Energy Level			
My Spiritual Life			
Adventures and Fun			
My Physical Body and Health			
Friendships and Social Time			

Chapter 17:

WHO ARE YOU?

When I was in fourth grade, my class put on *Cinderella*. My nine-year-old self was wildly creative and slightly hyperactive, so I immediately began daydreaming about being the star of the show. I desperately wanted to be in the spotlight.

However, when it came to actual school, I was shy. If I didn't understand a lesson from the day, I wouldn't ask. I would just guess. I didn't have a ton of friends but stuck closely to a handful I didn't feel scared speaking to. The shyer I was, the easier it was to be shy. In fact, other people began to expect that of me.

When it came time to audition for *Cinderella*, I deeply wanted the role. I would have even settled for an ugly stepsister. But I was *terrified*. How was I going to burst out into song and dance in the very same setting that always had me anxiously sweating bullets any time we were forced to read a paragraph out loud in English?

I practiced at home nightly for the role. My parents would clap for me and tell me how awesome I was. I was ready. When the day came of the audition, I stepped on stage, and my confidence quickly faded. I was catapulted right back into my shy school self. I put my head down and quickly whispered the lines. I opted out of the song portion, despite several weeks of preparation.

When the roles were announced the following week, I was cast as "Bird #2." *Not even Bird #1.* This role came with no speaking lines and a hideous, homemade yellow costume my mother somehow convinced me to wear again for Halloween the following year. *All the kids in the neighborhood called me Big Bird for, like, six months after that.* I, resentful, spent a full year side-eyeing the girl who did get cast as Cinderella.

My soul self had big dreams. But my belief about who I was at school stopped me from giving myself a chance to achieve them.

My point is we tend to stay steady in who we believe ourselves to be, even at the sacrifice of what we truly want. It feels weird and uncomfortable to step outside of who we see ourselves as and who we tell ourselves we are. Remember, our brains are out to gather information to prove our existing beliefs are correct. Our beliefs about who we are guide our behaviors, thoughts, and actions.

It is unlikely that someone who is prim and proper will be caught dancing on the tables unless, of course, they can blame it on the tequila. For a studious student, suddenly taking on slacker tendencies would create mental conflict. We call this distress cognitive dissonance.

Cognitive dissonance is the inconsistency between our beliefs and our behavior or attitude. This can also be when we hold two conflicting viewpoints at the same time. For example, you want to stop drinking but end up having a glass of wine at a dinner out with friends. Undertaking a major difference in our thoughts and behaviors often creates anxiety until either the belief changes to match the behavior or the behavior changes to match the belief.

When we are trying to change our life, we make the error of wanting to make a change but not yet believing we are someone who is capable of it.

If I identify as someone who eats chips and watches Netflix every night, it's a contrast to start working out every morning at 5 a.m. A 5 a.m. Peloton rider isn't who I believe I am. Unless, of course, I start to deliberately change the belief of who I am. In this scenario, our wording matters. Although we may not experience anxiety trying to work out, the belief is still guiding our behaviors and consistency. This means we are more likely to follow through if we begin to believe that's who we are becoming.

For example, look at the difference between these two statements: "I'm a drinker who wants to quit." vs "I'm a non-drinker." In one, you still identify as a drinker. In the other? You're able to identify yourself as someone who simply doesn't partake in drinking. You just aren't that type of person. If we consider how our brain is like a Google search bar, you can imagine what each of these identity filters has our mental programming searching for.

Assessing our identity is vital for true change. What parts of our person have we declared to be inflexible? What behaviors and personality traits have we dedicated ourselves to embodying?

At the end of the day, we have genetic components informing our lives, sure. But a good portion of who we are is more flexible and moldable than we give credit for.

As we start the process of claiming our comeback and stepping into the greatest versions of ourselves, we have to take an honest look at who we believe we are.

Our inner narrative guides our brain to action. Remember, we need to be dedicated in our efforts to reduce cognitive dissonance. Only then will your thoughts and behaviors fall into alignment with your innermost self.

This is epic news because we know we have the power to ease our change in who we are and how we act by creating new beliefs about our identity! We have the power to create new beliefs because beliefs are just thoughts we keep thinking. This means the pathway to a new version of ourselves comes with deciding what we want and who we desire to be and getting clear on what type of thoughts we need to believe to get us there.

I'm a firm believer that thoughts materialize into reality. *I'm a die-hard law of attraction girl.* Repeated thoughts can also become neural pathways. We want better neural pathways because they are the brain's messenger; they tell our body what to look for and what habits to engage in.

Forming neural pathways with repetitive thoughts is like carving a path in the woods with a machete. The more you walk and carve in the same direction, the easier it is to walk through. It's the same with our brains. The more we think about a certain thought, the more we carve that thought into our brains. Thoughts that are repeated enough become a belief. The more you think about something, the more your brain is likely to adapt and automatically think about it.

In order to change our lives and become the person we know we are capable of being, we have to create better neural pathways by choosing better thoughts about ourselves.

Maybe you've believed you are shy all your life. My question for you is, does this belief lead you to your best self? Do you get to be Cinderella, or are you going to settle for Bird #2?

One way I like to do this work is to look at my goals or desires and ask myself who I would need to become to reach these goals. I love using this affirmation: "I'm willing to believe I can be _____" and "I choose to be willing to believe I can show up for myself. I am open to believing I can follow through."

Designing your life starts with awareness of who you are and who you want to be. You have to understand how your beliefs shape your behaviors and get clear on what beliefs you've held that are hurting you. You can choose differently. You can always show up differently and better. You can go from someone who reacts to someone who pauses first, self-soothes, and then responds. You can go from Bird #2 to Cinderella. At any given moment, the beauty of our lives is we can rewrite our personality and our inner story.

My Identity Worksheet

Who people think I am:

_____

_____

_____

_____

Who I really am:

_____

_____

_____

_____

Who I want to be:

_____

_____

_____

_____

Thoughts that will help me become who I want to be:

_____

_____

_____

_____

Chapter 18:

IF-FIRMATIONS

Anything we've developed as a deep or core belief is just a thought we kept thinking. *How simple. How basic.* This means we can change almost *anything* in our lives, starting simply by shifting our thoughts.

But this can pose a challenge when our belief is so deep we can't imagine anything else being true. How do I force a new thought that I'm healthy when I've focused so frequently on being unwell? I don't believe it. I've thought about this for years. I've seen it. I've felt it. I've experienced it. How can anything else be true?

Your brain is super argumentative. Honestly, it's like a small child protesting broccoli at dinner. We like the thoughts we've created because we created them! They are familiar. While we find comfort in thinking the same thoughts, it doesn't mean that the same way is the best for improving your life.

I'm a huge fan of affirmations. Affirmations are "I am" or "I feel" statements that are used to shift old beliefs.

Instead of saying, "I am so sick," you would say something like, "I am willing to feel healthier every day."

As deeply as I believe in the power of affirmations, I also recognize that not all deep beliefs are willing to be moved so easily with a simple opposing thought. For example, if you're someone who has believed love is impossible for years, how could you possibly begin to believe love can happen for you? If the new thought you're trying to implement is too "far-fetched" (at least for where you are right now) or different from what you've believed forever, your brain will dismiss the new affirmation as bullshit. Envision your brain doing a patented teen eye roll.

But we're not quitters! We don't give up when our brain is being a dick. We find a way to make it easier.

Here comes if-firmations with a cape and a sword and all the possibilities! When we pose a new thought to our brains, we invite the opportunity to see something new. We can do this a little more easily by choosing different words to help us out.

Instead of going from "I am so sick" to "I am healthy" or "I will never find love" to "I've found the most amazing love," we can simply say, "*What if* I can be healthy?" "*What if* I can find amazing love?" "*What if* I can change my brain, and it's even easier than I thought it could be?" If you don't like the "what if," you might try *why* instead. "*Why* can't I be healthy?" "*Why* can't I find incredible love?" "*Why* not me?"

Your brain really just needs to feel open to new options. How does it feel to pose those questions? When we ask our brain a question, it automatically will search for an answer. This is why asking the right questions is vital. When we ask crappy questions like "why me?" or "Why does this always happen?" it's unlikely you'll receive feel-good answers.

The "what if" technique allows us to loosen the grip on our brain's deepened neural pathways. From a place of posing new possibilities, we can begin truly designing our life.

We can give our brain new suggestions and new commands, which will start to reprogram it in a way that is a better reflection of who we desire to be.

I want you to think of an area of your life you have a crappy, old, outdated belief around. Just pose the question, "*What if* it could be better?" "*What if* it could not only be better but could be incredible?" What would you have to believe about yourself to get there? It's totally possible! Play around with words that hold stronger meanings. Your brain will answer what you ask. Ask the right questions.

Chapter 19:

HABITS

When I was first moving to the Carolinas, Groupon instantly became my BFF. It introduced me to plenty of activities I wouldn't typically try, including aerial silks. Aerial silks are an acrobatic apparatus where a person dangles from fabric rigged on a ceiling beam. You often see them at the circus or at festivals.

Although I've never dreamed of running away with the circus, I was left in awe when I attended my first aerial class. Women of all shapes and sizes were entangling themselves in ribbons, lyra, and trapeze. They would methodically wrap themselves until they gracefully plummeted from the top of the ribbons, catching themselves at the bottom. I instantly decided I wanted to be one of these gracefully falling women.

The only problem was I had zero upper-body strength. Like, none. Grip strength was a missing feature in my evolution. *Which had always come in handy when getting out of moving furniture.* The instructor promised me that I would build these muscles if I were to commit to classes. I committed.

Over the last two years, doing a class a week, my grip and upper body strength have grown significantly. I've tried a few studios, made friends, and proven myself wrong about both my grip strength and what I'm capable of more times than I can count. I am able to do so many exercises in the air that were once a struggle to do from the ground.

Noticing something you'd like to improve on is important. You don't change by staying the same. Of course, I believe our thoughts lead to emotion, which invites action, but we can't *solely* rely on our thoughts to create a new life. We have to look closely at how we spend our time. Where does our day go? What is the ultimate result of each activity we take part in each day?

Our lives are composed of a series of activities that we do on a daily basis. These repetitive daily habits create our life. Brushing our teeth daily leads to clean, cared-for teeth. Drinking water daily leads to a hydrated, energized body. Engaging in loads of negative self-talk leads to feeling bad about yourself and your life. Each daily habit has a positive or negative result, whether we want it to or not. Take a look at what you spend your time doing. How much scrolling on social media do you do? Do the activities you do daily get you closer to your goals or further away?

When we look carefully at our habits, we can see what is gained from them. If I spend four or more hours a day on Instagram, what do I gain from that? Does it make me feel better or worse about myself? Our habits can become automatic and develop as neural pathways, like we talked about earlier. Unless we really stop and look at these habits, we may not realize why our lives are less exciting and fulfilling than we want.

When the New Year rolls around, most of us like to try on new identities and promise ourselves habits that we know would be good for us. But knowing something is good for us and *acting* are two entirely different things. I wouldn't have developed that grip strength without practicing each week. You're not going to develop inner peace or cultivate joy by filling your day with thoughts and activities that do the opposite. As we explore what we want for ourselves, we also have to ask the question: What habit(s) will help me get there?

When I was writing this book, I had a hard time creating space to get it finished. I knew that finishing this book before my thirty-fifth birthday was important to me, but I didn't have any habits in place to create the feeling of progress toward my goal.

One habit I consistently do is called a bullet journal. A bullet journal is a way of habit tracking by creating a daily bulleted list of to-dos to check off. For me, this typically includes working out, meditating, manifesting, and reading ten minutes of a personal growth book. At the end of each day, I go through and put a checkmark on what I've completed. This helps me make sure I'm doing the activities that make me a better version of myself. Knowing I wanted to finish this book, I decided to add twenty minutes of daily writing/editing to my bullet journal.

Obviously, you're holding this book in your hands, so we know this tactic was effective for me! Although I wrote and edited most days, there were days I didn't. Because life happens, kids have softball games or dance rehearsals, or exhaustion hits, and you may not always nail it. The purpose of having a bullet journal is to hold yourself accountable and guide yourself gently back to your intentions of what activities you know work for you and feel good. Don't judge when you miss a day; just give yourself grace and get back on track.

Now is the perfect time to ask yourself, what do you desire? What habits would you need in place to help you reach this goal?

First things first: Develop an awareness of your current habits. Monitor yourself by jotting down everything you do in a day. Brush your teeth? Jot it down. Scroll on TikTok? Write it down. Gossip with co-workers? Write it down. Once a full list has been developed, ask yourself if each of the activities moves you in the direction you desire.

If you're studying your list like, "Girl, I watch a lot of Netflix and am clearly pulling an unpaid part-time job on social media," it may be time to try something new. How do we create a new habit, though? What makes a habit stick?

I don't know if I can legally say this, but go buy *Atomic Habits* by James Clear. Run, don't walk. *He is the baby*

Jesus of habits. Atomic Habits is the most functional text on how to form new habits that I've encountered. I am going to attempt to do his work justice by summarizing a few key points here.

Firstly, Clear directs us to make new habits obvious. Declare your intention for this change with your new identity in mind. "I am someone who _____." This could be works out, has a ton of love in their life, and is successful. Fill in the blanks. Now create visual cues in your environment. This may look like setting out your workout clothes the night before, leaving your vitamins on the counter, or checking off your habits on a bullet journal to "not break the chain."

Another great option for forming habits is trying habit stacking. Habit stacking is where you pair something you'd like to do with something you already do. Try pairing affirmations or if-firmations with something you already do daily, like washing your face or applying moisturizer.

If you're trying to break a bad habit, Clear encourages us to make it invisible. Reduce your exposure. For example, I love soda—specifically, Dr. Pepper. I don't keep it in my house because I know I would drink it nonstop. For me, out of sight, out of mind is a tactic that works.

Secondly, *Atomic Habits* encourages us to make our new habits attractive. Pair your new habit with something enjoyable beforehand. Make a special Americano before sitting down to finish your project. Or join a culture that promotes your desired behavior, which adds to habit sustainability. Many people enjoy running groups or book clubs.

When trying to break a bad habit, you can make it unattractive. Come up with a list of reasons you're better without it. What are the benefits of releasing this bad habit? What are the risks of keeping it?

The third part Clear explains is to make it easy. Decrease the number of steps between you and what you want. If you want to work out in the morning, sleeping in your workout clothes could be a good start. I eventually switched to an aerial studio closer to my house to minimize the "too far away" excuse.

You can also implement what James Clear calls a two-minute rule, meaning you commit to your habit for a small amount of time to start. Maybe your goal is keeping up with laundry. Each day, you commit to only folding laundry for two minutes. We are more likely to stick to something that feels manageable. From that two-minute mark, we can build up to larger chunks of time. The ease of a smaller time commitment builds the habit and boosts our self-esteem while releasing the resistance of the "I don't have enough time" excuse.

If we want to make a habit unattractive or break one, we can take steps to get there more difficult. For example, a client of mine was trying to quit smoking. She agreed if she was going to purchase cigarettes, she was only allowed to purchase them from a store thirty-five minutes away. This gave her time between the craving and the action to truly think it through. Create obstacles between you and your usual bad habit.

Our daily habits matter, whether it's exercise, meditation, or beginning to change our thoughts. Repetition gets results. Make sure your habits are in alignment with who you desire to be. Take a moment right now to choose the habit that is best suited for you by exploring what you need most. More energy? Better mindset? Create a plan for when and how you will implement this one habit. Try only starting with one small habit at a time. Do not underestimate the power in building self-trust that comes with following through on only one small habit. From there, you can build on them. Make sure your beliefs are set up to be someone who follows through; watch the magic begin.

Bullet Journal Sample

WRITE YOUR IDEAS

WEEK OF

	SUN	MON	TUE	WED	THUR	FRI	SAT
EXERCISE	X			X	X		X
MEDITATE	X		X	X			
MANIFEST	X	X	X	X	X	X	
READ 10 MINUTES		X		X			
MOOD RATING	8	7	7	9	7	6	7

I'M SOMEONE WHO FOLLOWS THROUGH

WHAT I DID WELL THIS WEEK:

_____

_____

WHAT HABITS MAKE ME FEEL GOOD?

_____

Chapter 20:

TOOLS TO CHANGE YOUR MIND

If you've ever bought furniture from IKEA, you know that you can have all of the parts in front of you for a brand-new armoire and still be confused about where to start. Heck, you can even be mid-process, following directions, building the structure, and encounter a screw that's missing or a drawer that won't go on track.

Our comeback journey is like building IKEA furniture. I'm giving you a ton of different tools, but you must use your intuition of what tools stand out to you to try. Create awareness of what tools you're not ready for yet. We can also order extra parts to fill in the gap of what's not working. The tools in this chapter are like those extra parts.

Now that we know how deeply powerful our brain and habits are in creating a better life for ourselves, we can create intentional time to build and strengthen these mental muscles. This may mean setting a little alarm on your phone that pops up with your favorite if-firmation or revisiting who you believe yourself to be every morning or night. Making the way we think part of our habits will help us create consistency and lead to real change.

The more we visit what we desire rather than what we don't desire, the more we build new and better neural pathways. The more we build better pathways, the easier we will start to search for better in our world. I believe that everyone resonates with different tools that create their "a-ha!" moments and massive shifts. I've compiled a few other science-backed options for changing your mind just in case any pieces are missing in our comeback.

Meditation

I know the urge to skip this section. I used to believe meditation was for the birds, too! My brain would go a million miles an hour, and who was I to stop it? I mean, I couldn't if I tried. Or so I thought.

Every book you read will tell you there's a specific, proper way to meditate. That you have to sit a certain way, on a certain pillow, and then you're doing it right. I'm here to ruin that narrative. For me, meditation is the ability to bring my focus fully into the present moment. You're nailing it if you can do that, even for a minute.

Sometimes it feels like our brain is running the show, and we are just victims to its impulsive thoughts and whims. But meditation will train your brain to gain control over what Buddha describes as the "monkey mind."

Meditation has an absurd number of physiological and mental health benefits. According to a Healthline article by Matthew Thorpe, M.D., it has scientifically been proven to reduce anxiety and stress, increase self-awareness, improve focus, improve sleep, decrease addictive or impulsive behaviors, decrease pain, lower blood pressure, and decrease symptoms of depression.[21] So, why wouldn't you at least try it out?

To meditate, you are going to find a comfortable, safe space in which to sit or lie down. You can keep your eyes open and focus on an object or close them. You can set an alarm for a couple minutes. *You can build on the number of minutes later.*

Now we've actually already done this exercise earlier in the book; I just didn't label it meditation. *See, easy!* You're going to breathe in and follow the flow of air down through your lungs and back out. Letting your body relax a little more with each breath. As your brain starts to think of other things—it likely will, and that's okay—acknowledge the distracting thought and then bring your energy and focus back to where the flow of air is in your body. This trains your brain to not entertain every single crazy thought you have.

Again, even just attempting this for a minute a day to start is a powerful way to start changing your mind. True benefits of meditating come at building up to a minimum of ten minutes per day.

I want to point out that plenty of people find that level of quiet and calm stressful. They may do better with active meditation. Some find themselves in a meditative state when they are cleaning, running, swimming, organizing, or doing another kind of moving activity that allows them to clear their mind and be focused on the present moment and present task. Do what works for you.

Envisioning

Our brain doesn't know what is real and what isn't, which I think is one of the best and scariest facts about the brain. I mean, how do you think we are capable of panic? Our brain believes that our perception is reality, meaning we can signal our body into fight or flight solely based on thoughts and our imagination. Think of a panic attack; your blood is pumping, your heart is beating fast, and you are sweating and shaking. Often these can occur even in the safety of your own bedroom, with no present threat.

The good news is that if our brain is powerful enough to create all of that, we can use it to our benefit by envisioning what we want to change.

One of my favorite studies on the power of visualizing was conducted by the Lerner Research Institute. Researchers measuring finger strength encouraged volunteers to envision their fingers extending and contracting.[22] They also had a group that actually did physical extensions and contractions. Both groups improved in their original finger strength. What's incredible is the group who only envisioned doing the exercises instead of physically doing them improved finger strength by thirty-five percent!

So, you mean, just by envisioning something, I can grow a muscle or weaken it? The answer is a resounding yes! Professional athletes, especially Olympians, have been on the visualization train for years. They know the power of seeing themselves win the gold medal, become faster or stronger, or successfully make every shot on the basketball court.

How will this help you? First off, you can envision yourself as the person you want to be. The more detail with which you can create this visualization, the more you can connect a feeling, and the more your brain will respond as if it is already the case. Envisioning creates memories in your brain as though the thing you are envisioning has already occurred. It activates your chemistry as though what you're envisioning is currently happening, good or bad. If we can activate panicked energy, we can also activate calm energy by envisioning ourselves as calm and confident. What if we could visit this feeling and vision so frequently that it can feel like a memory?

Secondly, we can shrink major stressors. Have something that's holding you up? A situation you can't get over? Envision the situation in your mind and then envision it shrinking. Watch as it gets smaller and smaller until it's nothing but a little ant on the ground. So tiny you can't even pay attention to it. Notice how it feels to gain power over a situation that was knocking you down.

You also might envision unloading the energy of stress, anxiety, worry, or sadness into a box. You can then put a lid on the box and put it on a shelf or watch it drift away into space until it completely disappears.

Your brain is taking note of all the thoughts and experiences you have in your head. The more you play with the visualization practices, the more powerful you will feel, especially over the crappy stuff that has happened, and the more your brain will buy into the new visualizations you're creating as your reality.

Using Your Memory

We can fully envision something we want to become that we aren't yet, or we can dive into our memory and pull up a sensation that we are familiar with. I want you to think of a time when you were proud of yourself. A time when you did something you thought you couldn't do. I want you to see that day or moment as vividly and with as much detail as you can recall it. What were you wearing? What location were you in? What smells were present? What did it feel like? Who was there?

Our brain has no sense of time, which means recalling a feeling can make it feel as though that feeling is currently happening. This is why recalling bad feelings can feel like a punch in the gut, as if they are going on right now. But again, all that we can use for bad, we can also use for good.

Researchers in the UK in 2018 found that reliving positive memories, specifically of pride, worth, or social connection, not only helped reduce depression scores but also disrupted and reduced negative thought patterns.[23] How powerful is it to use our memory in a more productive way?!

Write down some of your favorite feel-good memories. Use this list when you're feeling off or low. Use your memory to help you connect to your positive memories and emotions to help shift your mood.

Changing Your Body Language

What if we can change our mood with our bodies? How are you feeling right now? How are you sitting? Is your chin up or down? Is your body straight up or slouched? Are you curled up or taking up space? Our body language impacts our mind more than most people realize!

Did you know depression has a look to it? In a mental health intake, there is a visual, physical assessment that helps therapists cue into someone's mental state. For example, someone who is depressed may look visibly disheveled or slouched; their eye contact is typically minimal, looking down or away. These ways of holding your body not only send signals to those around you that you're down but send signals to your brain that you're sad.

Yes, slouching, crossing your legs, and keeping your head down for more than two minutes can actually change your brain chemistry. Researchers from Colombia University Amy Cuddy and Dana Carney found that these body postures activate higher cortisol levels which are associated with depression and other mental health problems.[24] They also lowered testosterone. Testosterone levels are linked to confidence and assertiveness. Lower testosterone means lower confidence.

Did you know confidence has a look as well? Making eye contact, having good posture, and keeping your chin up are all indicators not only to the outside world but to your brain that you're confident. Cuddy and Carney also studied the impact of power poses, such as the superman or superwoman pose. *Think standing with hands on your hips, chin up.* They found that two minutes in this posture lowered cortisol and increased testosterone.[25]

Although this research was done on short-term brain changes, it may indicate that prolonged and intentional body posture could actually make a massive impact on our brains. This also means that you can shift your brain chemistry at any given moment by simply changing your posture. *I told you this could be easy.*

Another quick way to create a positive mental shift is by the way we get dressed in the morning. Perhaps you've felt off but have also been rocking leggings and a messy bun for the last week. Try putting yourself together and wearing your favorite clothing item or something that feels special. Choosing brighter colors can also boost our mood.

The moral of the story is that you have so much incredible power in your thoughts and mind. As our pal Spiderman says, "With great power comes great responsibility!" Play with what works for you. This may mean trying out different types of meditation, envisioning yourself succeeding or healing, pulling from good memories, or changing your body posture. You may feel called toward different techniques or tools in different seasons of your life. Give yourself permission to try them on.

PART 4.

THE PART IN THE LIGHT

The idea of reclaiming your power can be overwhelming. There are so many pathways to get there. There're habits to form and thoughts to change, but what if you don't have to do this alone? What if you can begin to trust your gut feelings and inner knowing? What if there's a bigger energy supporting you and guiding you?

Part of the work I've been immersed in over the last decade is sorting out the gaps in the healing process. Where are we getting stuck and why? What pieces of information, practices, or ideations would help improve our ability to feel better quicker?

While working in a traditional mental health counseling job, I realized there was a huge difference between those who made improvements and those who stayed stuck. Why were some people able to change their mind or life quicker than others? What is the common denominator amongst those who shifted into a better state quicker? Any belief in a kind and loving higher power. *Hear me out.*

No matter what your preconceived notions are about a higher power, the majority of people recognize that some things in life are unexplainable. Even Nobel Prize winner physicist Max Planck suggests gaps in science appear to only be explainable by force greater than ourselves: "All matter originates and exists only by virtue of a force which brings the particle of an atom to vibration and holds the most minute solar system of the atom together. We must assume behind this force the existence of a conscious and intelligent mind. This mind is the matrix of all matter."[26]

Neurotheologists, a scientific group that studies the brain and religion, suggest that the brain is actually hardwired to believe in a higher power. What if we are hardwired to believe in God? What if, even in science, there are gaps that cannot be filled in with numbers and logic? People across the country are more frequently acknowledging the presence of energy and intuition, using interchangeable words to relay the same intangible ideas. It has been said, "In religion, we call it spirit. In science, we call it energy. In the streets, we call it vibes. All I'm saying is trust it" (author unknown).

The Part in the Light promises to remind you that your comeback journey doesn't have to be just up to you and your own will. We get to explore ways energy may be impacting your progress and thought process while teaching you how to listen to your intuition. I will remind you of the magic of the Universe and clue you into the ways you're being divinely supported. Let's dive into a new perspective of spirituality and examine your personal beliefs.

Chapter 21:

WAIT, AM I...INTUITIVE?

About seven years ago, only a year or so into working as a traditional counselor, I realized I was picking up information about my clients that they hadn't told me. This ran deeper than observations you can make about a person from a physical or surface way. Suddenly, I felt incredibly aware of their biggest fears, insecurities, or deeper patterns. I'd point out these insights and they would reply, "Wait? Have I already told you that?"

This experience began happening more and more frequently. Being a logical person, I began to question why. Why was I able to be so in sync with my clients? How did I suddenly know the person's deeper desires? Was I *psychic*? And most importantly, was I losing my ever-loving mind?

After a long meeting with my boss, Christy, I knew I needed to get to the bottom of it. I began to deep dive into the exploration of intuition. Sure, I had experienced gut feelings before, but intuition in the sense of knowing information about other people was foreign to me. I was determined to understand. How do we intentionally activate our intuition? How can we learn to trust it?

My research landed me at what I jokingly refer to as "Hogwarts," a series of intuition classes held by a psychic medium nearby. Up until this point, I was amused by psychics but equally creeped out by them, similar to hearing scary stories that make the hair on the back of your neck stand up but never really knowing if it was real. However, something about this medium felt right to me. I knew I wanted to train with her to get a better understanding of how intuition worked and improve my trust in my own.

Through working with this medium, I learned that everyone has an intuition that is speaking to them. *You're no exception.* Your intuition is speaking to you about your surroundings, but more importantly, it's actively guiding you to make better choices in your life. Intuitive development is nothing more than a skillset, like learning to play an instrument or fine-tuning your baseball swing. Learning to hear and understand intuition takes practice. Trusting your intuition takes time.

My boss at the time was curious about my journey, having had similar inexplicable intuitive experiences in her own therapy sessions. In an effort to understand this more, we started to play intuition games back and forth with each other.

One day she set a rock on my desk. She simply said, "Tell me what you get from this rock." In the energetic world, we call this psychometry. Psychometry is the idea that all objects hold electromagnetic energy, and you can intuitively read information from that energy. I held this rock on and off all day. When I held it, my shoulders tensed. My head was filled with images of crumbling. A map of Europe flashed through my mind. Suddenly, I just knew this was a piece of the Berlin wall.

Shaking, I ran into Christy's office and said, "I don't want to be wrong here, but I can't help but feel like this is a piece of the Berlin wall." Her jaw dropped. She had been given the piece of the wall from a foreign exchange student nearly seventeen years earlier. Why would I know that? Like, seriously, how the fuck did I know that?

After that mystifying moment, I began to collect more evidence about my intuition. I wrote down gut feelings and coincidences. I wrote down synchronicities and deeper understandings. I dedicated time in my day to meditating and observing how my intuition spoke to me. I grasped how the energy of people, objects, buildings, and atmospheres impacted me and my clients and our mental health.

This understanding of my intuition and energy has been a saving grace, both personally and professionally. Discovering the role that energy plays in depression and anxiety not only helped me in my own life, but it allowed me to teach my clients techniques to address both the impact of their energy and mindset. *I'll share more on how to handle energy later.* Energy is often, in my opinion, the "sticking point" when it comes to changing your thoughts. We may want to change, but when we are trapped by energy, it will feel extra difficult to think of new thoughts or engage in new behaviors. I'll teach you how to shift this energy.

Discovering how my soul speaks to me and the impact of energy has been a superpower. It's also the best way I've found to make decisions that feel in alignment. As a reminder, alignment is when your head, heart, soul, and actions are on the same page.

As a former agnostic, I get this section may feel weird to read. I've been curious, yet skeptical, about spirituality since I was little. My Aunt Kim would record psychic Sylvia Browne on *The Montel Williams Show*, and we would binge it after school. Even ten years ago, I would have definitely brushed my very real intuitive experiences off as "woo-woo" and "too out there." I would have rolled my eyes, especially at the part about the psychic medium, because those were just fake entertainment, right?

Understanding took a lot of repeated "coincidences" and self-trust to believe and see my intuition was not only real but freakishly accurate. I required documentation for years to see how blatantly the Universe was speaking to me and supporting me. I kept a notes section in my phone of every intuitive thought or gut feeling I had to collect proof that what I was feeling was real. After a while, I had so much evidence that those intuitive nudges were valid and correct that I couldn't deny my intuition.

You may have some personal opinions about what is right or wrong, real or fake, within this topic. You may feel like you want to skip this section or even put this book in the donation pile, but I encourage you to keep an open mind and see what resonates. This section isn't about teaching you to become a psychic or to push religion or any belief. It's to help you recognize how to hear your soul speaking to you. Because it is, all the time. To clearly see the impact and influence of positive and negative energy around you. Learning intuition means learning to make decisions from your soul for your best and highest good. To help you see your life and circumstances from a different perspective—a loving, expansive one.

I encourage you to take the information I'm presenting here and see where it might fit you. As with *all* information you encounter, take what resonates and leave the rest. You come equipped with an intuition, a guidance system. Your job is to be willing to listen to it.

Chapter 22:

HEARING YOUR INTUITION

When getting clear on who you are, you'll start to hear something in you, guiding you. Getting aligned with your truest soul self is a key component to your comeback. Alignment is the practice of quieting all of the external noise to hear your internal truth and guidance, then acting on it. Getting aligned comes quickest when we begin to seek to hear our intuition.

Intuition will often sound like your own voice because it is. However, your intuition is a wiser version of yourself. We all experience our intuition differently. Some people identify it as a vibe. People can feel it emotionally or physically. Some people see pictures or movies in their minds of what might occur or what's possible. Others just have a deep knowing. However you experience it, our soul comes equipped with an internal GPS guiding you through your life to your best self with turn-by-turn directions.

Everyone has intuition. I'm not special, and you're no exception to that. Think of it as the quiet whispers of your soul. It's an inner nudge or pull toward the right path, experiences, and people. The challenging part is to learn how to hear it.

You don't have to be a professional psychic to be able to read energy. Whether it's the sleazy vibe you just got off your Uber driver or an interview for a dream job that suddenly feels *off* in your gut, our intuitions are constantly providing us with information about ourselves and our surroundings.

Have you ever had a situation you knew wasn't right? Chances are you talked yourself out of feeling that way because why would you not like the new hire? But then it happened: she stole money from the cash register. Or you had a gut feeling you had that your boyfriend was cheating on you, and you finally found proof in his pants pocket. That too-good-to-be-true car you bought broke down. The business partner you warily let in ended up bad-mouthing you to loyal clients. And you freaking knew it! Why didn't you listen to your instincts?

We are taught at a young age to follow logic instead of intuition. We are taught science, facts, and evidence are required to make our choices. Mainstream culture impresses on us to follow the trail of science and logic, leaving our gut response as secondary guidance. Some people even mock the idea of intuition, and energy, making it seem foreign, "out there," and taboo.

Logic definitely has its purpose and place in our lives; logic is part of our learning brain. It's the part that has previously gathered information on what's already been done or experienced. Logic loves evidence and facts. The more tangible and numbers-based, the better! However, sometimes we use logic to override our gut feelings.

Malcolm Gladwell discussed this idea in his book *Talking to Strangers*.[27] In one chapter, he talks about the people who knew Hitler, sharing that many leaders initially had a bad feeling when first meeting him. The deeper people connected with Hitler, the more they were confused by his actions. Many overrode their initial gut feelings with "evidence" that he wasn't as bad as they'd initially thought.

Leaders like Neville Chamberlain were easily won over after spending time with Hitler. Noting he seemed "not crazy, but determined," Chamberlain described Hitler as a man who had a strong, friendly handshake. How could a determined man with a strong, friendly handshake be evil? We know how history went from here.

Although Gladwell's book isn't necessarily about intuition, it does strongly imply the accuracy of our gut feelings. It also expresses how easily we can talk ourselves out of trusting our initial gut feeling with logic.

The most important thing we can do for our soul's alignment is learning to understand both the function of our logic *and* our intuition and strike the proper balance.

Intuition isn't pre-planned or pre-known information. It's a calm knowing at the moment, without conscious reasoning. Intuition could be something like the pull or random thought to take a different route than I-77 even though Waze hasn't detected any slowdowns. You override your intuition and say to yourself, "Well, I-77 is the fastest route." You get on it anyway, only to find yourself sitting in traffic for two hours.

Our highest self speaks to us through our intuition in subtle ways. For example, your eyes might get drawn to a certain word or message while scrolling through your social media and it's exactly what you need to hear at that moment. Or you might feel called to check one more time even when you swore you've scrolled through every last house in the listings, only to see you somehow missed the house of your dreams. Intuition is the subtle "Here you go, this is what you've been looking for." The "aha" moment. A love note from the Universe, if you will.

What's interesting is we can't *think* our way into intuitive knowing. We have to learn first how our own intuition speaks to us. *Hint: Meditation is a great gateway.* Second, how to trust it. Third, how to ask for it.

Logic accesses the limited information we've already acquired, only searching through what is already known. As we discussed earlier, survival mode is staying in our logical brain, only accessing limited information. Survival mode only pulls from what is already known or directly in front of you and typically comes from feel-bad energy like fear or anxiety. In survival mode, we are more likely to fill in the gaps with our negative narratives and deny our intuition.

Whereas intuition, although still in the moment, opens us up to the unknown, inner divine guidance, showing us possibilities, opportunities, or calm truths about situations we can't see yet. Survival mode feels limited and fear-based. Intuition feels calm and open to possibilities.

When we *stop* thinking about or obsessing over the answer, we can tap into our highest selves more easily. Our intuition is loudest in our resting state or spaces where we are on autopilot, like showering, daydreaming, or driving. This is due to our brain frequency being in a more relaxed alpha or theta space. When our brain frequency is at an alpha or theta level, our imagination, visualization, creativity, inspiration, and insight are heightened. Our intuition is most easily accessed when we are relaxed. It is hard to hear our intuition in survival mode because our brain is amped up, prepping for fight or flight.

When we are stressed out, we might find ourselves trying too hard to "figure it out." Thinking about the situation or problem over and over again. Obsessing about a problem puts us into limited thinking and survival mode, blocking our intuition and forcing us to look only through information about the situation that we already know. Just because it's known doesn't mean there aren't other potentials, ways, or options. Finding a more calm or relaxed mental state invites our intuition to show us all of the possibilities. Including our intuition in our decision-making opens us up to think outside the box to solve our problems with ease and creativity. Our logic is finite, and our intuition is infinite.

Intuition is in and of the moment. If you feel a call to inspired action, listen to your intuition right then and there. It's important to do it the moment you feel it. For example, if you're driving along and suddenly feel a deep need to call your uncle, you'd better pull off to the side of the road and give him a ring. Intuition doesn't wait. It's a collective push from the Universe while it's pulling all the other strings to make situations align. You can't ignore the lengths the Universe is going to for you by not listening to it.

How My Intuition Speaks to Me

You might be wondering how to go about unlocking this important higher-self feature. Good news! We all have the ability to intentionally access it. *Clairs* are the names for our extra senses, which is the way your intuition communicates with you. You can have multiple clairs or one strong one. Here are some ways you might already be experiencing your intuition:

Clairvoyance – Clear Seeing. This is for the person who experiences their intuition by seeing an image or movie in their head. Maybe you see a conversation play out before it actually does. *Déjà vu, much?* Maybe you get a flash of a closed restaurant only to drive there and realize the restaurant is closed for a private event. Yep, our intuition even speaks to us about non-fate, non-exciting things.

Clairsentience – Clear Feeling. This is a popular one. Clear feeling is the ability to feel or take on other people's emotional or physical feelings and the energy of a place or object. We also call this being empathic! Clairsentient people often have trouble in a large crowd because they find themselves taking on the energy of the whole. I have a whole section on empaths coming up that you're going to want to read, especially if you're identifying with being clairsentient.

Being clairsentient/empathic is being in the room with someone sad and suddenly feeling sad, even if you felt fine before. The trick with clairsentience is assessing your energy and emotions before and after. How did I feel before I walked into this old building? How am I feeling now? How do I feel when I leave?

Clairsentience may also feel like a gut feeling. You may be able to physically pinpoint the intuition in the form of your stomach feeling off. This may feel like a pit in your stomach, butterflies, or even nausea.

Clairsentience also may take the shape of physical ailments. You may have physical problems that come and go with no real explanation. Many people who have been diagnosed with fibromyalgia or other inexplicable disorders are often incredibly intuitive and can manage their symptoms by understanding and learning to clear their energy. I will detail how to clear energy in the next chapter.

Clairaudience – Clear Hearing. I'll be the first to say that if you're hearing voices telling you to do bad things, you need to get that checked with a psychiatrist. Intuition doesn't cause distress. It's calm, not paranoid or fear-based. Even if you know something isn't meant to happen or isn't going to work out, you'll initially feel calm. Intuition comes from a calm knowing that surpasses our mind and human fears. Your fear is not intuition.

Clairaudience may show up as hearing a song in your head on repeat. What is the meaning of the words in the song? The key with intuition, especially when it comes to clairsentience, is it needs to be random. If a song you haven't heard in a couple years randomly pops into your head, this is different from a catchy song you just listened to. It's worth checking out the lyrics to see how they resonate with your life circumstances or if there is a helpful message in there. You may hear ringing in your ears which may signify paying attention to what is happening or what you were just thinking. You also may have a lot of back-and-forth conversations in your head, as though you were talking to a wiser version of yourself. These conversations will feel different when it's with your higher self. Often the messages are wiser, in the third person, or more loving than how you typically think.

Claircognizance – Clear Knowing. This one is tricky and harder to learn to trust than any of the other clairs. This is intuitive information that you just know. You don't know why you know. It won't make logical sense or have a trail of thoughts or evidence leading up to the knowledge.

This is the predominant way I experience my intuition. I've grown to trust it over the years because I've watched how absolutely right it is every time I listen to it. How do I know this dude my friend brought to dinner is garbage? I just know. I'm not processing a feeling, thought, or vision of it. I just know.

Intentionally Connecting to Your Intuition

This is really important. Don't skip this part. There's a lot I don't believe with regard to good and evil, but I do believe low vibrating energy exists. I believe energy is on a scale from high to low. This is the vibration that energy frequencies radiate at, which is where we get the term high vibe. High energetic vibrations closely match the feelings of love, joy, and God. Low energetic vibrations match the dark, heavy stuff like deep depression, anxiety, and fear. I think it really matters what energy we are using and surrounding ourselves with at all times, especially when tapping into our intuition.

When you use your intuition by asking for it to come from God, the Universe, your higher self, or the light, it feels easy and free-flowing and leaves you feeling good and aligned. Your intuition is always speaking to you, but as you become aware and more open to listening to your highest self, you can be more intentional. Flowing energy from a lower energy source or negative intention may leave you feeling tired, irritable, or not feeling like yourself. Your intuition should leave your physical body feeling light and your heart hopeful.

Some guidelines I adhere to:

1. **Invitation.** Ask for help. Whatever you believe in as a higher entity, now is the perfect time to invite that in. God, Angels, and Universe, please guide us to receive only helpful and healing information. Please show us the next right step on our path. Please guide us during the process, not just in our problems.

2. **Intention.** An intention is what you want to feel or desire to occur. I set the intention out loud or in my head to be guided to what is in my best and highest good. I only invite information from my soul, my highest self, that is healing, helpful, or otherwise preventative. The point of our intuition in this book is not to "read" others but to learn to hear our own guidance and begin to trust it.

3. **Write it down.** When we set the intention to receive intuitive information for our best and highest good, we may receive it as an aha moment, intuitive nudge, or knowing. Write them down. You can even write down vivid dreams. Create a notes section in your phone or journal to create evidence for the accuracy of your intuition. I always feel like when we do this, the Universe sees us listening and says, "Oh hey! This one's paying attention." It allows you to see more easily where and how your intuition speaks to you. You may also notice patterns, times of day, and activities

where your intuition is more noticeable to help you identify and hear your intuition more clearly.

The Difference Between Feelings and Intuition

How do we begin to differentiate between our soul speaking and feelings based on fill-in-the-gap negative narratives? I'm glad you asked! This one can be a little tricky at first. People are most commonly focused on their feelings, which isn't a bad thing. Feelings are the way we know something needs to change. Change is easier when we are noticeably uncomfortable.

However, feelings alone can keep us stuck in a mental and emotional loop. Our neural circuits form when we repeat a thought which leads us to repeat the same thoughts creating the same feelings over and over. Unless something breaks that circuitry. Intuition is the guiding force of action to our next level and a circuit breaker. Let's explore some differences between how feelings and intrusive thoughts (sudden worries or fears) might show up versus our intuition:

- Intuition is a calm, loving, and nurturing voice. Intrusive thoughts are often fear-based.

- Thoughts are often logical. Intuitive thoughts often feel like, "Why was I thinking about that?"

- Thoughts have a progression—a trail leading from one to the next. Intuition comes out of nowhere, often in a moment where you weren't thinking about that particular topic.

- Intuitive thoughts are often quiet—a subtle noticing or nudge. Intrusive thoughts are often repetitive and loud.

- Intuitive thoughts feel helpful, like expansive possibilities. Intrusive thoughts make you feel stuck, scared, or small.

- Intuition presents wise, loving information from your higher self. Feelings often come from an internal narrative of desperation, insecurity, or lack, our subconscious filling in the missing gaps.

- Intuition comes from a deeper place inside of you—it will often feel soul level. Intrusive thoughts usually come from your head.

Your intuition from The Universe can feel like magic. But it can only help you if you listen to its guidance. Oftentimes people hear their intuition and don't trust it. They second-guess themselves. Listening is the important part. That's where shit changes for you.

The Universe cannot and will not force you to do something you don't want to do. We have free will and a boatload of it. This means sometimes we can pray and pray and pray and still be standing in our own way. Maybe we're not ready yet or don't want to do what we know we must. Maybe we don't believe in ourselves enough to chase that bigger dream our soul is guiding us to.

Whatever the case, your soul is a GPS. You can follow the gentle turn-by-turn directions, or you can go your own way and hope there's no construction or dead ends. The choice is always yours. By recognizing your dominant senses, you can begin paying more attention to how and when your intuition speaks to you. Differentiating this calm inner voice from fearful thoughts takes practice but will ultimately help you make better, stronger, and more aligned decisions. Write down the nudges. Collect evidence for your intuition. Let your higher self be your guide during your comeback.

Chapter 23:

WHEN YOU FEEL EVERYTHING

When I first moved to South Carolina, I connected with a lot of different people in an attempt to make some new friends. I had one friend in particular whom I adored. She was beautiful, sweet, and fun to be around.

I want to start this story by acknowledging I've always been pretty comfortable in my body. I work out, eat relatively healthy, and despite recognizing my body isn't model-like, it's been so good to me. My body size has never been a daily focus for me. However, the more I hung out with this friend, the more I felt insecure about my size.

When I was around her, I suddenly felt massive. I felt self-conscious in tighter clothes. I was hyper-aware of what I was eating, despite never having watched my calorie intake or restricted my food. I didn't realize it at first, but I was only feeling this way when I was physically with her. When I was home by myself, I was back to loving my curves and not thinking about my weight.

After a few months of noticing this feeling on and off, I started to dig deeper. What about this friend made me feel insecure? Why was I getting triggered about body issues when I previously never focused on them? There was no logical explanation. And again, these thoughts and energy weren't part of my day-to-day; they were only present when I hung out with her.

One Friday evening, after some late-night cocktails, she confessed to me that she had an eating disorder she was battling. She explained how she always felt massive and insecure. She expressed to a T all of the thoughts and feelings that I only experienced when I was with her. At this moment, I realized I had been taking on her energy, thoughts, and feelings as though they were my own.

Has this ever happened to you? Maybe you went to dinner with a group of people, ordered a meal, only to get it and wonder why you picked it? Your friend admits they had been craving it, and you realize you were picking up their energy. A friend of mine was taking care of her father after surgery. She was having severe stomach pain, which instantly stopped once he admitted how bad the pain medications were making his stomach feel.

We are consistently and constantly reading energy, whether we recognize it or not. This is what makes us empathic. When you are watching *The Notebook* and crying because Noah wrote Ally 365 days in a row with no response, you're crying because the same neurons that fire in your brain when you feel rejected or lost are firing by simply watching a loss or a rejection. These neurons are called mirror neurons, and their job is to go out into the world, collect information, and come back to fire the same neural receptors in our brain as though it were happening to us.

Mirror neurons help us understand people and connect with the world around us. When we can empathize with another person's situation, we respond more appropriately, creating feelings of support and connection. There is a debate amongst scientists on whether mirror neurons are an evolutionary feature. Some believe that mirror neurons developed to assist our socio-cognitive functioning, while others believe their development is completely individual and dependent on sensorimotor learning.

The downfall of mirror neurons is that they often pick up on everything even when we're not trying to. For example, have you ever been at the store and suddenly felt irritable for no reason at all? Or maybe you are sitting at home and feel a rush of anxiety. You reach for your phone and see your mother has been trying to reach you about her car breaking down. You picked up her feelings of anxiety even when she wasn't in the same room.

A recent Nobel Prize awarded to Clauser, Aspect, and Zeilinger for Quantum Entanglement suggests there is something faster than speed of light: the information that travels between two particles.[28] This notion may be helpful in furthering our scientific understanding of how and why we experience energy.

Being an empathic person, in my opinion, is a superpower. We know what our friends need. We can tell someone's not okay without them saying it. However, it doesn't always feel like a fun feature when our brain is firing emotions that aren't even ours. We can end up feeling tossed around by everyone else's thoughts, feelings, or intentions.

Recognizing that feeling you're experiencing may not be your own is *so* important. When making our comeback, we can do all of the mindset work, but if the energy is still blowing us over like a palm tree in a hurricane, it can be really hard to move on or manage your thoughts and feelings in a consistent way. This doesn't mean that *all* emotions or thoughts you experience aren't yours. But if you're doing the mindset work, challenging past beliefs, and not getting far or doing all the back-to-the-basics work or mind tools and don't seem to be seeing any benefit, it's worth exploring if energy is playing a role.

Ways to recognize you might be taking on someone else's energy:

- Your thoughts feel obsessive or unable to be moved, even by coping mechanisms that typically work.

- You were feeling fine earlier, and out of nowhere, you feel depressed, anxious, or overwhelmed.

- Thinking odd thoughts that simply don't feel like yours.

- Random coming and going of aches, pains, stomach aches, headaches, and other physical symptoms.

- Extreme focus on someone else or feeling "stuck" on a conversation or incident that occurred.

- Feeling you're "not yourself."

This doesn't mean we just accept taking on energy as our normal. We aren't victims of the energetic field or the world around us. We're actually fiercely powerful creatures with the capacity to step back into our power when we recognize we're being impacted. Learning how someone else's energy may impact your experience is helpful in reclaiming your power. There are a few important solutions to managing your energetic field in case you find yourself bogged down by energy:

1. **Get to know your own energy.** Go out for a hike or walk by yourself. Turn your phone off or delete social media. This may just be for a day, or you may feel called to disconnect from social media for a month or more. Create a healing space in your home that feels the most like you. Time alone and intentional disconnection will help you know what your energy feels like.

2. **Put away your phone.** Energy can be received both in person and through technology. Disconnecting from social media helps you stop plugging

into the energy of hundreds of people a day. Be protective of your energy in this way.

3. **Recognize what you are feeling or experiencing may not be your own.** Simply posing the question, "Is this mine?" can often help create a separation between you and the energy. It may feel lighter or moveable afterward.

4. **Ground your energy.** Walk barefoot outside. Create a grounding visualization, like a cord connecting the core of the earth to your tailbone. Breathe up from your feet like they are straws connecting to the earth. Try walking through the woods or spending time barefoot outdoors. If we think of an oak tree in a hurricane, it's grounded in the earth and isn't going to fall over with the intense wind. If we think of a palm tree, it's unstable and likely to get blown around by the wind. Be the oak tree.

5. **Clear your energy.** You can do this by moving your body. Visualizing white light pouring over you. Meditation. Using clearing tools like sage, "holy wood" known as palo santo, or healing crystals to clear yourself or your space. Setting the intention for your energy to be protected. Taking an Epsom salt bath.

6. **Be intentional.** If you can feel bad energy, you can also be intentional about surrounding yourself with good energy. Put on music that is upbeat

or has a positive message. Watch inspiring videos of people with the energy you'd love to feel. Do what feels good. Pay attention to what feels good.

Why am I talking so much about energy? Because I need you to understand its role in your healing and feeling stuck. Intuition isn't just the ability to hear your soul's guidance. It's the ability to "read the room." It's understanding how you may be impacted by others energetically and being intentional about separating, protecting your energy, and standing strong in your own energy, so you're overall less influenced by other lower vibrations.

If we consider that our mirror neurons have the potential to make people's fear, doubt, or sadness feel like our own, we want to ensure we are doing what we can to keep our energy clear and on the higher end of the energetic scale, as I discussed earlier. On the scale, we can assess what energy we are in simply by our mood. Good or neutral mood? Our energy is in a good place. Low or bad mood? Our energy needs to be tended to. This may include setting boundaries or removing people or situations from your life. This may look like committing to an energetic ritual, like an energetic visualization or palo santo, as part of your morning routine.

Right now, my biggest recommendations are to practice clearing your energy and taking inventory of how you feel day to day as well as before and after you spend time with places and people. If you're feeling super stuck despite doing the work, ask yourself if there's any energy blocking you? Pay close attention to getting to know your own energy by finding time to spend alone. Create a habit with detoxing rituals like Epsom salt baths or meditation to help you get a better sense of that. Remember, you can move and change your energy at any given point in time.

Chapter 24:

JESUS WORKS WITH MY DAD

I grew up in the suburb of a city known for its prison in a small little corner of Upstate New York. My elementary school was conspicuously placed on the hill directly behind the prison. As in, you could see the brick of the building from our play yard. The air was regularly potent with the stench of cow manure from the farm that was managed by the prisoners. This smell permeated the air during spring recess.

If there's one important detail you have to know about me, it's that I was a real badass on the monkey bars in third grade. *I know, be jealous.* For me, recess was a solid thirty minutes of breathing in the manure-filled air while gliding easily and effortlessly from one end of the monkey bars to the next. My favorite part? Climbing on top of the bars to flip myself upside down, dangling by my knees. *There's no blood rush like that blood rush.*

One day, when multiple classes were gathered together on the playground, I was doing my typical dangle when I had an acquaintance from another class, Debbie, flip down next to me. I distinctly remember the little girl looking over at me and saying, "Have you been saved by Jesus Christ, or are you going to hell? Because my mom says you might be going to hell, and I shouldn't play with you."

If I'm honest, I didn't know who Jesus was or where on the geographical map Hell was placed. *So, as you can see, this isn't a chapter on religion.* I was puzzled but did the only right thing I could think of, and on the spot, I made something up about Jesus being friends with my dad. *Sounded legit at the time.* I went home that day and asked my mom if I was going to hell.

My often bizarre or harsh encounters with religion throughout my childhood left me confused. I was convinced, as a kid, that everyone associated with religion had lost their mind. This isn't my current take on faith systems, but that's just another example of how your past encounters with anything, let alone a higher power, do not have to define what feels right or true to you now.

As I grew older and met more Debbies from the monkey bars, I knew I needed to get to the bottom of this whole idea of religion. At first, I did it out of curiosity. How could all these people with different faiths believe so deeply that their view was the right view?

In my early twenties, I bought every book I could to learn more about Judaism, Christianity, Catholicism, Hinduism, Islam, Taoism, and many more. As someone who grew up lacking a connection with religion or a higher power, I decided the best way would be to study all of them and their commonalities. Everyone claimed to be "the" one to follow…so which one was it?!

What I found spending years digging through historical texts was this: All religions have a few major pieces in common. Through structures and rituals, they are how people organize their life, trust in a higher power, and shape their behavior. The majority of religions pray or utilize some form of intentional thought. Most importantly, a higher power is used to explain the unexplainable, both the miracles and the madness.

I'm not telling you to go get baptized! I'm just telling you to consider, if you haven't already, that nothing is an accident. Seeing evidence of the intangible on a daily basis when I was learning my intuition forced me to consider that maybe, just maybe, there really was something "bigger" out there. I use the word God, Spirit, and Universe interchangeably because I'm not referencing religion; I'm speaking directly of faith in something bigger. *You can replace my terms with ones that feel right to you.*

The world is marinating in magical synchronicities and inexplicable déjà vu moments. We can fall victim to what seems like chaos, or we can begin to pose the question, is there something bigger at play? *What if* the world is intentional in how it works? *What if* bad stuff didn't happen simply because the world is shit? *What if* everything was working in intricate order? I believe deeply if your spirit woke you up today, it's a sign there's still more here for you.

It wouldn't take you long to research incredible miracles of people who walk after being paralyzed for half their life or people whose tumors healed nearly overnight. You could study the wild similarities in near-death experiences. You could pay attention to how vast the sky is, dive into the wildness of space, and explore the depth of the ocean. Looking at the bigger picture, it's hard not to wonder if there's something more.

Although I've never structured my spiritual beliefs in a specific way, I want to share a little about what I believe, in case it resonates. I believe that we are extensions of God's energy. Each of us has a spark of the Universe in us. That the energy of our highest selves, the core of who we are, and the Universe is the energy of pure love. I believe we get glimpses of possibility from our highest selves through our imagination, and our intuition is just a pathway of communication. In the moments we feel most like ourselves, we are aligned with love (our divine essence), God, and our highest selves. I believe the Universe is for us, not against us. When something is taken away or lost, it creates space for something new to enter.

I believe we have a soul family. People who feel familiar to us who have signed up to come here and connect with us to help us become who we are meant to be. They will help us learn lessons that will let our souls grow to their full potential. I believe intention is a guiding force in our day and that we are co-creators with the Universe of our earthly experience. I believe our divine purpose is best expressed when we are fully, authentically ourselves.

I don't know if I believe the old adage that everything happens for a reason. What I do believe is without meaning, suffering is just suffering. I like to look at faith this way: You can be a victim of your life events. You can wallow in them. You can feel like there's no rhyme or reason. But then you're using your precious time here on earth just feeling shitty and victimized. *Or*, you can feel the shift of energy that comes along with believing in a bigger plan. You can look for the magic. You can dig for purpose or reason. You can watch the unfolding. Essentially, faith is a tool you can choose to use or not use.

When we feel miserable and heartbroken, it's helpful to return to the idea that every event can be processed from a different perspective. Although we can't go back and stop the terrible thing from happening to us, we can choose to be curious if there's a purpose and explore how we move forward from here. Our responsibility lies not in what happened but in what we do and how we choose to live our lives after.

Might we also consider: what if an event is simply protecting us from something? What if your black hole breakup is what leads you to try kickboxing, introducing you to your kickboxing instructor who would become the love of your life? This is a perfect moment to explore your past. Look at situations you prayed would work out yet are now grateful they didn't.

The magic of believing in the Universe comes down to the idea that you don't have to figure it out alone. You have a bigger force on your side. If you're feeling weak and hopeless and are only relying on the way you feel at that moment, you're eliminating the exponential power, possibility, and influence of the Universe.

I've found that with many clients, as I begin to introduce the idea of energy or the Universe, people seem to have this recognition within themselves. As in, learning about the Universe feels right or true to them even if they don't consciously understand why. Afterward, they seem calmer, more optimistic, and more able to release the tight grip on their negative thoughts or feelings. Perhaps it's that hard wiring in our brain, the neurotheologists suggested.

My recommendation in all of this is to encourage you to find *something* to believe in. I'm not Debbie from the playground, so I won't tell you what that has to be. Nor will I tell you something bad will happen to you if you don't.

Perhaps the Universe already has a natural order of operations. We can apply that to our own lives. When we try to control our situation or other people's behaviors, we're just tampering with it. We're creating resistance between where we are and who we are meant to be.

Faith is a cognitive process. Sometimes it will be easy. Some days, you'll be able to read this book and say, "Nichole's right!" Maybe the Universe and our lives are on purpose. As author and spiritualist Gabby Bernstein would say, "The Universe has my back." You'll feel divinely supported and have an underlying knowing that the hardships are shaping you into your best self. And some days, you'll want to put this book through a woodchipper and tell me to eff off. *Either is fine.*

Faith is like a muscle you work in the gym. You can't do one rep and end up with a six-pack of faith-abs. It's a process of choosing to return to the information you connect with, whether that's a religious text, a book by author and spiritual guide Wayne Dyer, a YouTube video by manifestation "money queen" Amanda Frances, or surrounding yourself with friends who spiritually uplift you.

I don't think faith can be handed to you or pushed on you—I think you get to decide for yourself what feels most true. Because we know the truth, our truth, deep down. What feels good inside of us when we say it. What makes the most sense to you in your alignment.

Finding your power in your comeback is remembering you're not alone. The entire Universe is supporting you and guiding you. Explore what you believe to be true about the Universe or God. You get to decide for yourself right now what feels most right to you. You get to play with research and try on beliefs. Continue to know you are wildly and divinely supported.

Chapter 25:

GOD, ANGELS, UNIVERSE: GIVE ME PROOF

As "woo-woo" as I am, I also love science and evidence. I'm a girl who is very into "proof." Which is why I so deeply believe in what I'm sharing. I've acquired enough personal proof the Universe exists. I want to share one of my favorite God moments with you.

When I was finishing writing my first book, *Rock Your Soul,* I chose a tiny little cabin in Vermont to spend a couple days wrapping up editing. On the way back from Vermont to New York, I felt the pull to hike a trail in the Adirondack Mountains by myself.

This didn't seem like it would be a huge deal until my scroll through Instagram the night before led me to pictures of bears on the peak I was planning to hike. My confidence in my solo hike faded. I started to worry about what would happen if I saw a bear. Would I be able to telepathically tell it to fuck off? Would I befriend the bear, and would we ride off into the sunset together?

Then I started to panic that I may have now manifested bear sightings or worse! *Please don't eat me, Mr. Bear.*

My anxiety in approaching this hike was higher than normal. The next morning, on my drive from Vermont to the mountains, I decided to reset my energy and rewrite how this would go. I decided to manifest a wonderful hike full of beautiful scenery, cute, *safe* animals, and a feeling of confidence and freedom. After all, I was equipped. I had a trail map. I had snacks, water, and great trail shoes. I had a compass. A compass I didn't actually know how to work, but that's beside the point. I trusted both myself and the intuitive nudge calling me to go there. God wouldn't call me to the mountains just to have bears eat me, right?

When I entered this hike, I was immediately engulfed in a swarm of gorgeous yellow butterflies. It felt like a fairy tale, and I knew it was a sign I was going to be just fine.

The Indian Head trail in the Adirondacks (ADK) is eleven miles long, and it starts out on a flat, safely paved golf course road, followed by a shift into steeper terrain. Although it's not technically considered a peak, it's one of my favorite views in the ADK. As I turned to fully enter the heavier forested area, it dawned on me that I had already hiked about three to four miles without seeing or hearing another person. That made sense—it was mid-morning on a Thursday during blackfly season. A time of year avid hikers tend to avoid where swarming, biting black flies are in high population. The quiet was unnerving, so I jingled my keys and sang loudly to myself as I walked…because, you know, *bears.*

The heavy rainstorms from the night knocked down many trees and muddied the paths. The ADK needs to step up its trail marker game if you ask me because between the fallen branches blocking what would have otherwise been clear paths and runoff creating perceived trails that weren't actually paths, I soon found myself lost from one trail marker to the next. Everything felt very unclear. Y'all, I was lost in the mountains of the Adirondacks alone. Well, not alone…because *bears.*

I didn't immediately panic. I was resourceful. I was smart. I tried to retrace my steps to the last trail marker. But after twenty minutes of retracing, I didn't know if I was even heading the right way back anymore. *Then* I started to panic. What the hell had I gotten myself into? Hiking alone in a place I had never hiked before…with bears? Why was I so weirdly confident about things I was not familiar with? Who does this? My head filled with doubts, and my heart raced as I realized my phone had not even one bar of service. My eyes welled up with tears. *Don't mind me, just a lost girl, crying on the side of a mountain.*

I tried to slow my breathing and get my mind right. I looked directly up, staring at the trees enclosing a patch of the bluest sky. I remember saying out loud to God, "Now would be a really great time to help me believe in you. Like, not a day from now, right now. I'm lost, and I need help."

Within a minute of my extremely desperate prayer, for the first time during my entire hike, I heard voices. Not the crazy kind, just in my head! The kind coming from a group of sweet elderly women who were hiking the same mountain. Using their voices as my guide, I found my way back to the actual trail.

I thanked the sky for its quick reply and asked the women for directions to get to the Indian Head Lookout. They laughed and told me they were heading there, too. They extended an invitation to finish the hike with them if I didn't mind their slow pace. I, recovering from my recent meltdown, agreed that would be great.

During our last few miles up the mountain, I learned these women were over eighty and hiked a mountain every single day. They shared their stories of winter snowshoeing and sliding down the mountains on their butts. In the ADK, if you hike all forty-six peaks, you are considered a "forty-sixer." These women were forty-sixers, several times over.

I learned a lot that day, about myself, about these women, and maybe most importantly, about God. That was the very moment all doubt or maybes around the Universe left my system. I was supported. I was loved. I was being carried, in every moment, even in the ones I felt extremely lost. I just had to be willing to invite in guidance.

Because I didn't develop any type of relationship with a higher power early on, it took me a while to figure it out. I won't claim to have figured it out for anyone else but me. I will point out that as I get older, this viewpoint is continuously evolving and growing. Your relationship with the Universe is deeply personal. You get to go back through everything you've been told about it and assess what feels aligned for you. However, I am always willing to encourage people to try techniques or practices that have allowed me and my clients to feel more supported and connected.

When I first started believing in God, the Universe, Spirit, I used this connection in desperation (i.e., on the side of a mountain.) I accessed it superficially at first, only when shit really hit the fan. But the cool thing is the Universe is accessible at all times. Source energy is dying to support you. Even when sitting down to write this book, I whispered, "Show me what they need to know."

Of course, we have free will. The Universe would never intervene unless you were moving super off track from who you're truly meant to be. This may come disguised as an out-of-the-blue big life event like an unexpected divorce or being let go from your safe and secure job. This may also look like everything slowly shifting to make the comfortable less comfortable, like a new boss who's a jerk. Everyday intervention from the Universe requires an invitation. A request. A prayer. An intention.

Sometimes, I truly don't know who I'm addressing. Like I said, I use the words interchangeably, all referring to this energy of love and support I believe exists. But I've learned to invite the Universe into the process, not just the problem. What if you were willing to be guided?

What if this guidance helped you understand what you're worthy of? What can you truly have in your life?

I love sending a request to God early in the morning to show me who I need to be today. You can send it out loud or in your head. I truly don't think it matters. "God, Angels, Universe, please guide me to be my best self today. Show me what to say, what to do, and how to be my best self. Help me be the best and highest version of myself in my deepest desires and authenticity." This is a take on the popular prayer from the channeled text *A Course in Miracles*.

I even invite this energy during client sessions or with projects. What would you have me do? What's the next right thing to say? When we start asking, we also start listening. This is a perfect chance to be intentional about connecting with our soul, intuition, and our source.

I believe the Universe speaks through our intuition. It's that knowing, that nudge. For me, that's God. That's your highest self, who knows better than to text your ex after three Jack and cokes. When we invite in help, a lot of times, we will experience the help through our own voice and in our own head.

You may not hear, feel, or experience anything right away. You may notice shifts in your mood throughout the day or "aha" moments. You may just feel more supported and loved. You may see signs like repeating numbers, feathers, or a certain knowledge that something or someone on the other side has your back. You may notice something falling into place a week from now. That's the important piece of being supported—we can ask for it but can't decide how or when it shows up.

If your miracle doesn't happen this very minute, it doesn't mean the Universe has forgotten about you. But it may mean you could use practice in patience, surrendering, and trusting it all gets to work out. You wouldn't plant a pumpkin seed then immediately stomp on the ground and give up on it turning to a pumpkin if it didn't grow right away, right? Because we know good things take time and trust. Same goes for inviting in the Universe.

As we are changing our lives, we can develop a connection with the Universe. When we start listening to our divine thoughts instead of our crazy ass intrusive thoughts, that, my friends, is when your life truly changes.

When you start following those GPS directions from your soul straight to your highest potential. You start listening to the truth of the highest version of you that you're worthy and loved. That you're supported and cared for. Your vibration moves up that energy scale. The heaviness fades. This is the access point to the most incredible experience. Your power is in listening to that inner voice and remembering the insane power you hold as an extension of the Universe.

Some people will refuse to believe in the unseen. They will go on with their ordinary life, blaming ordinary people for their ordinary annoyances. And that is totally fine. In the event you choose openness instead of ordinary, that's when life begins to feel a little more like magic.

PART 5.

THE PART WHERE YOU CREATE

I needed to get you here. I needed you to both learn and unlearn. I hope I've helped you recognize some truths, detach some rules, create awareness about the power of the mind, and understand a few basics from the spiritual world. This is the part where we mix the mind's power and the soul's magic to create your new life.

Ta-fucking-da! You've arrived!! This is the Cinderella part. The fairy Godmother stuff. I mean, no one's just going to hand you a dress and a carriage, but we're handing your *mind* a magic wand of information to help you collaborate with your soul and the Universe. You deserve to not only recognize your brain's power and the Universe's power but to truly step into your own!

This is my favorite part of the comeback process. The part where you get to design the ultimate version of yourself and your life. This is the section where you decide who you get to be and what you truly deserve. The part that promises you tools to really step into your destined spot as co-creator of your reality. I hope you're just as excited as I am because we're about to change your life.

The more we step into your future, the more the shit in the past will feel so small. The more you work with the Universe, the easier it all gets. What do you say? Ready to jump like Mary Poppins into the sidewalk creation of your new life?

Chapter 26:
THE MAGIC

I recently had a client, whom I will call Megan, who was burnt out. She desperately wanted to quit her nine-to-five job to start a coaching business. In one of our sessions, we explored what it would take for her to make this change. She laughed at me, stating, "My husband would have to make double the money for me to pull this off." With this concern about income and maintaining a comfy lifestyle, she felt a real change was impossible.

I responded, "Okay, so *what if* your husband made double the money?" She gave a semi-sarcastic, "I'm sure that would be nice." *I could feel the eye roll.* I encouraged her to direct her energy toward possibility, staying open to options.

Over the next few weeks, I challenged her a lot. We explored where her beliefs and limitations came from and how they were blocking her.

Megan began to shift her belief from "it's impossible; I'm stuck here forever" to "*what if* it's possible?" Staying open rather than deciding she was stuck put her in a position to receive divine inspiration from her intuition. She changed her thinking from a stuck mindset where nothing could be different to a mindset that included what ifs, challenging limiting beliefs, and intentionally looking for the magic.

Soon, she found herself experiencing more happiness and hope in her day to day, despite still not loving her job. We worked together and kept her energy clear through the use of regular Epsom salt baths, prioritizing getting outdoors. Two months after our initial call, she sent me a text that said, "I have big news."

At our next session, she didn't even let me say hello before shouting, "You're never going to believe this, but my husband got a promotion and will be making double his salary. I'm quitting my job next month!"

You guys didn't think I would make it this far without merging the way our brain works and the Universe, did you? When we begin to change our perception, improve our energy, and listen to our intuition, we invite the Universe in to help create pathways to what we desire. We call this manifestation.

Guess what? Your comeback is not just entirely on you and your own willpower. The Universe is on your side. Divine energy has a bigger, better blueprint than your finite mind could ever dream up. The Universe has infinite plans that counter your limiting beliefs about what's possible for you. This is the part where I get to remind you that you are divinely and wildly supported. You are so freaking loved. You are blessed and highly favored. You are an extension of the power that creates worlds. Your job? Is to remember that.

I believe deeply in the power of the brain. *Deeply.* The basics of how our brain works, filters, and sees the world had to come first in this book. For my science-based, logical people, I know you needed that understanding. Now I've got to take these ideas to the next level and go a little "woo-woo" on your ass.

In 2018, Gabriela Reyes Fuchs did a TEDx talk called "Rethinking death to understand life," where she showed images of cremated human remains under a microscope.[29] What was surprising about the images is they were bright, colorful, and nearly identical to a galaxy. So much so that the images could easily be mistaken for photos taken by the Hubble telescope.

While you might be saying, "That's weird and kind of gross," it's also a beautiful reminder that perhaps we're composed of the same stuff as the Universe. *What if that's correct?* That the galaxy, the damn *Universe*, is inside of us? Research conducted on the atomic makeup of 150,000 stars in a 2017 study by Sten Hasselquist of New Mexico State University proved that both stars and humans are made up of 97% of the same kind of atoms.[30] *Meaning: you are mostly stardust.*

If we are taking these studies into account, it's safe to pose the idea *what if* you're not just part of the Universe; *what if,* you *are* the Universe. I deeply believe we are an extension of the power that creates worlds. *What if* during your day all you had to do was remember that?

The question then becomes, what will you choose to create with your Universal power? The choice is yours. With your brain in a more helpful place plus the frequency-matching energy of the Universe on your side, it's time to create the life you truly deserve.

You are the great alchemist of your life. You are powerful, capable, and qualified to live the most incredible existence as your best and highest self. Maybe that doesn't feel true at the moment, but take a moment to consider it. *What if* you are?

Energy cannot be destroyed; it can only be transformed. This is the part of the book where we take the absolute garbage you've been up against and light that shit on fire. We're going to morph it into everything you're destined for. We are going to change the energy of insecurity and level it up to your divine confidence. We can release the past, knowing it's nothing more than the old energy we once experienced.

I can't sit here and force you to believe in magic. Some people just aren't on board. But what I know firsthand is that realizing changing my life wasn't just my own willpower but also a power within me connected to the Universe's energy and intelligence. That knowing is what took my life from a place of being broken and in despair to feeling an amount of abundance that's still hard for me to comprehend. From not wanting to wake up to feeling excited to come down the stairs every morning to my gorgeous home and manage my career and businesses where it never feels like I'm working.

Manifestation is a combination of your mental thoughts *and* your electromagnetic energy to create an undeniable frequency in your physical experience. So, how do we play with this idea to work not only with our mind but play with the Universe?

Remember, our brain doesn't know what's real and what's imagined. The Universe speaks through our intuition, but also, we have the power to create something new by using our imagination. Spiritualist Wayne Dyer said, "Everything that has existed was first imagined, which means that everything that will exist must first be imagined." Our imagination is our gateway to creating. It's also a preview from our highest self into the possibility of a new life and a new version of ourselves.

My journey first started with the book *The Secret* by Rhonda Byrnes. This introduction to Universal energy is simple yet powerful. The premise is based on the law of attraction, stating that what you put out into the world mentally returns to you physically. You attract into your life what you focus on through your thoughts.

Remember how we discussed that our brain looks to confirm what we think? And on top of that, our souls and bodies are energetic frequencies. Both our bodies and our thoughts hold energy, as does everything in the Universe. This means the situations we involve ourselves in have a frequency, and our desires have a frequency. The Universe creates an energetic match with our personal frequency to the physical situations, experiences, and things. *Good thoughts bring good things.* You might think this is total bullshit, and I thought so too at first, but hear me out.

The first challenge of *The Secret* urged me to consider *what if* instead of expecting bills in the mail, I expected checks? It seemed so far-fetched. At the time, I was still diving deeper into debt with my master's program. I was pregnant with my second child, already supporting a toddler, and couldn't afford to have my thermometer above 66 in an Upstate New York winter. Who would send me checks? Where would they even come from? No one was trying to hand me money. Everyone was just trying to collect it when I didn't have any to give. Even going to the mailbox felt overwhelming and filled with dread.

I suspended judgment for a week and went ahead and set the intention that I was willing to believe I could start receiving money in the mail. The thought of receiving checks felt so silly, but part of me was willing to play the what if game. *Curiosity is one of the most powerful components of change. What if* it worked? I thought about my intention only a few times before forgetting. Three weeks later, I received a $500 check in the mail. There had been an audit done on a business I'd worked at six years prior. As Matthew McConaughey says, "Greenlight!"

There were times after I began incorporating manifestation when I would believe in it and see more frequently how my thoughts impacted my physical life. There were also plenty of times when I felt doubtful or used my fear to control my life. Being willing to believe I'm connected to the Universe was a way I was able to maintain an openness to manifestation, a *what if* viewpoint. *What if* this actually works? *What if* I am a co-creator of my reality? Certainly, I would create something better.

Although my major changes happened over the span of several years, I attribute where I am to understanding and utilizing manifestation. Looking back, I can clearly see each step where the Universe was supporting me in the ways I was asking it to.

For the next few years, I continued to play with the Universe by asking for small shifts in my life. Small checks kept showing up for no real reason. People who owed me money from years ago started coming forward and offering to pay their debts. These small shifts led to bigger shifts. If I could receive checks, what else could I do for my mindset, my career, and my marriage?

Job opportunities presented themselves for both my husband and me, offering us more financial security. A free preschool program we were originally waitlisted for opened up, taking the place of the $16,000 a year we were spending on daycare. With more security came the ability to think differently about myself and the future. Not only that, I started to work my way out of my insecurities and depression through my manifesting. I decided I could be a little more confident every day. I decided I was worthy of a good life. *My creative mode was finally unlocked.*

I began to believe more deeply in manifestation every day. As usual, I set out to learn as much as possible. My life suddenly felt like it had an element of magic. For the first time in twenty-four years, I felt like I was in control of co-creating my future, not just falling victim to my daily circumstances.

I don't tell you this story to push some sort of "get rich" scheme. Manifestation is far deeper than that. I share this because my first experience with manifestation was tangible. Perhaps my logical brain needed physical evidence first to begin to see how the power could translate to the intangible. Maybe it had to happen this way so I could teach you all that the real power of using these tools and strategies in changing how we feel on the inside.

The truth is, we don't have to do this alone. We don't have to change alone or figure out every detail of how to get from point A to point B. There is a higher power playing a role in your life. There's a big beautiful, supportive energy wanting you to be your best self. An energy powerful enough to instantly shift situations, moods, and experiences. When we take personal responsibility for our thoughts, habits, and coping, we can invite the Universe in to shift the parts we can't figure out. You and the Universe are collaborators. You are stardust, after all.

I won't tell you that manifesting came easy after feeling so doubtful and negative for so long. *I still work on it.* I won't tell you that manifestation is an instant magical solution to your problems. *You're still responsible for your life.* I won't tell you that manifesting means you don't need to do the intrapersonal work, take action steps, and change the way you see yourself and the world. But I will tell you, our thoughts are powerful, and the Universe is ready and waiting to play with you if you're willing to suspend disbelief.

My manifestation skills have evolved far past asking for checks in the mail. I've realized manifestation is an embodiment of energy (your mood plus your perspective.) It's okay to feel skeptical; as long as you have the willingness to do the work, to be open or curious, the Universe will do its part. Keep in mind, your mindset shifting also allows your brain to see new opportunities. But any small shift in your energy moving up that energetic scale puts you in a better place to receive.

Do all of our manifestations emerge? The quick answer is no. We don't get everything we want. Sometimes we want things that are not in our best and highest good. I've come to recognize that some of our desires are too small or fear-based for what the Universe has in mind for us. Like that guy you knew was no good for you but really wanted a relationship with, the Universe knows there's better out there. The Universe is always looking out for our highest self, which means you have to trust not only in your manifestations but what shows up in your life, too. Patience is our bestie.

What if we suspended disbelief for a moment? *What if* we played with the Universe? *What if* we tried it on? *What if* we invite in opportunities for more? More excitement and more money? More love and more joy? *What if* we begin to see the magic not just in our thoughts and personal responsibility but in how the Universe effortlessly and consistently shows up for us? Combining care for our energy plus a mindset shift is where we truly begin to create something new for ourselves.

Chapter 27:
WHAT CAN I MANIFEST?

Anything! All areas of your life and all desires are manifestable. Sure, most people and social media accounts promote the manifestation of the physical, like manifesting the checks, the cars, and the vacations, which are a lot of fun. However, the more powerful thing, in my opinion, is a manifestation of smaller moments. Putting it out there that the meeting you're worried about with your boss will go better than expected. Intending green lights on your drive when you leave a little late. Manifesting invitations to connect with like-minded people when you're feeling lonely. Your relationship with your spouse improving daily. Your daughter's theater audition going well. Having an easy and fulfilling Monday. Believing your mood and energy level will be high for the day. The manifestation I'll advocate going for the most regularly is how you feel about yourself, your own self-perception, and self-love.

Manifesting my mood was a huge starting point for working my way out of depression. When I first started,

I couldn't truly buy into the belief of a life where I wasn't sad all the time. I couldn't even begin to envision it for myself. The doctors and therapists told me I was and would always be. Genetics or something. They were professionals. They would know, right? I believed I needed to accept my depression as the truth of what they had decided I was and what my future would be. Genetic? Generational? A permanently shitty malfunctioning brain and brain chemicals? Was this my only truth?

My first step in shifting out of my depression was deciding that the sad-forever story didn't have to be my truth. *What if* I could feel happier? Although, I know the power of the brain and will always preach it. I believe deeply that for some people, in order to shift out of a super low frequency or to disrupt really rigid patterns of dedicated, crappy thoughts and neural pathways, they may need to explore antidepressants or antianxiety medications. This isn't the best or right choice for everyone. But this is something that temporarily benefited me in the thick of my sadness, and it absolutely helped get me to a place to be able to truly entertain new thoughts.

A recent study done by researchers at the University College London in July 2022, Molecular Psychology, suggests that our age-old belief that depression is a chemical imbalance may not be accurate.[31] A review of this study by neuroscientist Andrew Huberman explains that it may be more of a neural circuitry issue rather than a previously thought chemical imbalance. This is actually great news![32]

When we pose new suggestions, create new thoughts, and expand our beliefs, we are disrupting neural circuitry, which may lead to the ability to pull ourselves out of a sad mental state, depression, or anxiety with a change in our mind alone. At least for me, I can say my doctor's diagnosis that my sadness had to be forever was incorrect. Depression wasn't a life sentence. Although it took getting very intentional about my life, my mind, my soul, and my energy to build my way out. I always wonder, what if I had accepted their story as my only truth?

What anyone else has decided you are does not have to be your destiny. Studies of the Universe, the brain, and deeper research into epigenetics like Mansuy and Mohanna's May 2011 study, *Epigenetics, and The Human Brain: Where Nurture Meets Nature*, have helped determine that our environment, energy, and relationships may have just as much influence, if not more, on our state of being and mood as our genes do.[33] In fact, your gene expression can be influenced by your environment and your mind.

This is all to say no one gets to decide for you who you get to be, what has to be true for you, and what mood you get to have. In most cases, you are not a victim of your personality. I began to see how my thought patterns were impacting my mood. Although I knew I wasn't willing to believe I was a confident powerhouse, I was willing to pose the if-firmation, "*What if* I could feel a little better every day?" I was willing to be open to a new perspective. I was willing to see traits to love about myself.

My confidence was growing every moment of every day. *Small shifts.*

When we start to manifest who we are in the world and how we love ourselves, everything shifts from there. Remember earlier when I discussed the importance of keeping your energy clear? This is because our energy is the frequency that draws your manifestations in or pushes them back.

Think of your energy as a ten-story building. The basement is for the garbage, our bad feelings, thoughts, and moods. In the basement, we find trash, rats, and old stuff no one really wants. Basement energy equals attraction of basement experiences and creates momentum around basement thoughts. As we get into a better mental and emotional space and think better thoughts, we begin to take the elevator to a better floor. Each floor we rise up to, each positive shift in energy, has cooler and cooler shit. The better the energy, the better quality we attract. We want to go for penthouse energy, a butler, and some Cristal.

Your mood and attraction point as a ten story building

What floor are you on?

Good Mood - Penthouse

Joy/appreciation/love

Passion/enthusiasm/optimism

Hopefulness /contentment/boredom

Pessimism/trustration/overwhelm

Dissapointment/Doubt/Worry

Anger/Revenge/Jealousy

Insecurity/Fear/Depression

Bad Mood - Basement

Adapted from the Emotional Guidance
Scale created by Abraham Hicks

When we love and accept ourselves when we choose to reach for a better feeling each moment, that is our power. That is our penthouse. When we hit a higher vibration and work towards being authentic, we are in the ultimate place and energetic frequency to be a match for the Universe's gift of top-level experiences, people, and situations destined for us.

Although you can manifest anything. I'd recommend starting with yourself. *I know, checks sound way more fun, but...* How do you want to walk through this world? How do you want to feel day to day? How do you want to experience your relationships? What kind of energy do you hold? What does your best self do? Dress like? Experience? How is she/he in each situation? Envisioning this for yourself is such a beautiful place to start. This shift will not only inform your brain on what to look for, but it will also alter you energetically and allow the Universe to support you in the best way possible, clearing paths to your most desired possibilities. *How cool is that?*

You can manifest anything. You are only limited to your imagination. My suggestion will always be to prioritize your manifestations around how you feel. This is where your true power and connection to the Universe will feel the most impact. Anything is possible from the space of self-care, self-love, and a better mood.

Chapter 28:

HOW TO MANIFEST

Fun fact: You're manifesting all of the time. Manifestation is simply the way we think about the world and ourselves. Every thought shapes our reality. Similar thoughts create a similar reality. Sort of like chewing gum two days in a row, there's no new flavor. But new thoughts? That's where the flavor comes back and the magic happens! Each thought holds a vibration that goes out to find its situational match energetically. It's a request to the Universe to help bring you your desires.

We must use our thoughts wisely. All of the affirmations and if-firmations we've already discussed are part of manifestation. You can use them. Practice daily by writing out your intentions for how you want your day to go. Remember, an intention is just a decision of what you'd like to feel and what you'd like to happen. The more time we spend on good feelings, thoughts, or visualization, the more power they have.

The first step of manifestation is to get really clear on what you want. This may mean writing down what your ideal job would look like. It's good to get specific if you feel clear about what you want. What hours would feel nice? Would you work with a team or solo? Would you work in a nice office or from home? How would this impact your home life? How would you feel coming to work? How would you feel during work?

If you don't feel clear, you can manifest in a way that is a little vaguer. What is the general feeling you'd like to have in this area of your life? What are you willing to believe is possible? What would you like more of? What would *more* look like? You can manifest by asking questions and answering them in any area of your life.

The key to manifestation is getting clear on how you want to feel in the new situation or scenario. How would you like to feel in that new house or driving the new car? How would you like to feel in that relationship? How would you like to feel getting that project finished as well as while creating it? How would you like to feel in your own skin on a daily basis?

Intentionally spend time in the energy of what you desire. Including manifestation in your day could look like taking a few minutes to visualize how your meeting is going to go at the beginning of the day or writing down affirmations of how you'd like to feel in the evening.

My favorite manifestation tool I've been using for the past decade is a letter to the Universe, similar to a gratitude journal. *Finding gratitude is a very high-vibe practice.* Every morning, I write a thank you letter to God, Angels, the Universe, my higher self, or whatever resonates. I write a letter as though everything I desire has already happened, and I'm just saying thank you for it. For example, "I am so grateful to feel so confident and light throughout my day. My kids are happy and healthy. Thank you for helping me make them feel loved, seen, and heard. I'm so relieved today's meeting went so well. I truly felt heard and received all of my feedback in a positive way." I've included an example at the end of this chapter.

As I am writing, I might feel intuitively pulled to connect with a person, look at a webpage, or jot down an idea that pops into my head. Writing, especially in cursive, gives us access to both our intuition and our creativity, according to a 2012 study.[34]

You can write as much or as little as you wish. You can write about anything in the present or future. Again, I suggest you include how you'd like to feel. I typically write, "It's safe to be myself. The more I'm me, the more the right people love me. I feel so content and purposeful in my life. I am so grateful to feel energized and productive today." This technique is also one of the ways I connect with God in the morning. This is a little reminder that I'm not on my own throughout my day. We're co-creators, after all. I recently found some of my old manifestation journals and realized that almost everything I once wanted is now in my existence.

I believe the Universe doesn't understand negatives, so instead of manifesting "I don't want to be overweight," you might try, "I feel confident and healthy in my body. I am so grateful for how my body supports me. The kinder I am to my body, the kinder it is to me. The kinder I am, the more my body's shape shifts to feel in alignment with who I truly am." When manifesting, look to speak life into what you want to occur rather than what you don't want to occur. I met a hiker in Utah on a trail once and was discussing my anxiety in steep drop-offs with him. In his words, "Look where you want to go, not where you don't want to go."

Another manifestation technique is visualization. We can use visualization, as we discussed earlier, to shrink negative memories, but we can also use visualization to imagine a version of ourselves and our life that is exciting.

Spend time visualizing who you desire to be. Include all of your senses. What perfume does he/she wear? How do they hold their body posture? What features can you notice or create in this version of yourself? How abundant are you? Remember, your brain has no idea what is real and what is perceived. Spending time and energy on the feeling of already having what you desire makes your brain begin to believe it is already true.

An underrated technique I will mention is alignment. Something that makes you a total magnet to your desires is also getting into alignment with yourself. Remember, alignment is making sure your thoughts, feelings, and actions match. Make sure you're getting really honest with yourself and those around you. Alignment and self-love are the highest frequencies we can access, which makes us at a high attraction point to what we want. They are the quickest elevator to the penthouse. What if manifesting comes easiest by just taking really good care of yourself? Intentionally treating yourself with kindness and love? *See, I told you this could be easy.*

Although it can be easy to look at your reality and feed energy into what already is, it's vital to keep your energy on what's possible not just what is known. Remember, your current circumstances are just your past manifestation brought to life. Which means what you're creating and manifesting now, you'll see in your future.

Think of affirmations and if-firmations as mental exercises and manifestation as spiritual exercise. If you have the willingness to believe or imagine something new, you have the power to create it. Although there are various ways to manifest, my personal favorites are writing a letter to the Universe and visualizing my dream self and dream life. Be intentional about getting into alignment, honoring your highest self, and really, intentionally loving yourself.

Daily Letter to the Universe Sample

January 10

God, Angels, Universe,

It is now January 10. I am so grateful to feel so energized and productive today. I feel confident in my skin and am fully myself in every situation I am in. I feel divinely supported. Everything is always working out for me. Today's meeting went so smooth and I felt so well spoken and well received. I feel inspired and motivated. I am so grateful my girls are happy, healthy, and feel seen, loved, and heard. We have such an incredible relationship. I choose to step into my greatness now. I choose to receive all the love, support, fun, and abundance. I was made for an incredible life. I choose to receive it now.

Thank You,
Nichole

Chapter 29:

RELEASING THE HOW

Many extremely successful celebrities like Oprah Winfrey, Will Smith, and Ariana Grande are known for being vocal about their belief in manifesting. In a 2011 interview, pop superstar Lady Gaga openly reported that prior to her fame, she would repeat the affirmation that she was famous several times daily.[35]

One night, Gaga was performing in a burlesque show and was discovered by R&B Singer Akon. I don't know her personally, but I anticipate she wasn't manifesting with the "how" in mind that Akon would have to arrive at a burlesque show on the designated day and time in order for this to happen. Instead, her belief that it was possible, her inspired action, and her alignment of performing helped create the right circumstances and moment. In one single moment, anything can change for the better.

Your job in manifestation is not to figure out *how* something you desire has to happen. Unlike the Universe, you have limited knowledge of every possibility. If I had started thinking too hard about who would send me checks or specifically how much money on my fixed income would come, I would've never been able to figure it out. Those possibilities weren't in my awareness yet.

This is why releasing "how" your manifestation has to show up for you is *so* important. The Universe and its possibilities are infinite. Every moment is a chance for anything to happen. Every single moment could be life-changing. You don't know what you don't know. That's what makes manifestation feel magical.

When we don't release "how" our manifestations have to happen, we shift into our logical brain, searching through limited knowledge of what can happen. Trying to "figure it out" invites our brain to only look for options we're aware of; it doesn't leave as much room to hear our intuition or see the magic of the Universe come in.

Trying to figure out "how" blocks you from receiving. Especially if you are only looking for what you desire to come from one place, one person, or one direction, you may actually miss your manifestation by having blinders on. Releasing the how means manifesting and setting intentions without deciding what routes you can receive them.

Releasing the "how" means truly trusting that the Universe knows how to create pathways to your desires. Trusting that it knows possibilities you can't see in your current physical world. Lady Gaga would have never been like today, I am going to perform at burlesque, and Akon, specifically, will walk in and discover me. This is the magic of the Universe. When we are aligned in who

we are, doing what we love, while believing in possibility, the Universe carves paths to what we desire or brings
something even better.

Chapter 30:

INSPIRED ACTION

When I first started my own intuitive therapeutic business, I had the tiniest office in the history of tiniest offices. I split this six-by-eight office with my business partner, Christy. She had the office Tuesday and Thursday. I had it Monday and Wednesday. This windowless nook was tucked in the way back of an old building. Starting this business was a risk and scary. We were so grateful for our micro office, specifically the price. As our schedules quickly filled up, we both began to feel we were outgrowing the space.

Christy and I sat down to manifest-write for a different space at an affordable price. We envisioned windows, an office that had space for both of us, and a price that made it feel easy to take the leap. One day as I was writing for this new space, I felt intuitively called to check in with our office manager, Steve. Steve told us that a new office in a newly remodeled building had just opened up to be rented, and it was only $100 more each. This new office space was exactly what we needed, with three offices and a waiting room. Moving into the new space gave our business the expansion we needed to make our business a full-time venture.

Manifestation isn't lazy. We can't sit on the couch, deciding we'll meet our soulmate if we never leave the house or take part in any action that will help us get there. I suppose there's always a chance our house catches on fire and a hot firefighter saves our ass, but let's not bet on that. We need inspired action!

When we create the manifestation and set the intention, we also have to listen to the pull or nudge of our inner guidance, our intuition. This may look like manifesting more clients in your business and feeling suddenly called to make a vulnerable post on social media. Or when manifesting your dream home, feeling pulled to drive down a street you haven't been on in a while and fall in love with a house you end up buying.

I love the action of manifestation journaling for this very reason. Sometimes when I am writing out my desires, I will feel a call to action that feels very clear. Writing in high-frequency energy, in a place of desire and gratitude, is a gateway to hearing our next aligned step. Keep in mind the ways you personally hear your intuition when it comes to listening for inspired action. Create intentional time to focus on being in the moment where we can more easily hear our intuition.

Remember, intuition is typically in the moment. The more aligned with our highest selves we are, the easier it is to hear it. But make sure to act in the moment you feel the urge—before you miss the wave of energy culminating in your favor!

Chapter 31:

RELEASING RESISTANCE

For half of my life, my grandmother lived with me. She ended up on disability and eventually went bankrupt. When she finally was able to move out, she moved into a 500-square-foot house my father fixed up. Despite not having much, she was the type of woman who was always giving as frequently as she could. Our Christmases typically consisted of small, thoughtful gifts or homemade vinyl-woven boxes.

On one of her last Christmases, she gave me so many highly priced gifts. Present after present, I was in shock at how much she spent on me. I kept telling her it was all too much. She needed the money more than I did. Tears streamed down her face as she told me she loved me, appreciated everything I did for her, and wanted to treat me. I was very concerned about how she was funding this extravagant Christmas.

A few months passed, and I got a call from my uncle that my grandmother and some friends had gone in on a lottery ticket and won $7.5 million. Although my grandma chose yearly payments and passed away before seeing most of her winnings, it's still a cool reminder that any moment can change your life, even in your seventies.

Now you might be thinking, "Nichole, you must always play the lottery." My answer? Despite seeing someone win, I don't personally believe I can win. I still have a ton of resistance around it. Winning the lottery wouldn't be an ideal manifestation for me based on my lack of belief that it can happen to me. What I know about resistance is if I have a huge block between what I want and my willingness to believe it, I'm less likely to be able to manifest it.

Remember when I was talking about how we can internally feel when we are willing to believe a thought or not? When talking about manifestation, we refer to this as your resistance.

When I say manifest $1,000 more a month, your brain or body might have a specific feeling. Perhaps you fully believe it, and a swirl of excitement arises. More than likely, your body is rejecting the idea of receiving $1,000 more a month, your heart may sink, your stomach might flip, and you may even notice energetic heaviness around your heart or body. This is how we know the belief is too big and we need to build up to the belief instead of deluding ourselves. If this is the case, we need to break the belief down. We might try $600, and if that feels like too much, we scale down to $200. The idea is we keep going down until we find something we feel internally *willing* to believe can occur. These are our set points—our lows and the highs of what we believe is a possibility.

Set points aren't good or bad. They just help us become aware of limiting beliefs and what we are *willing* to believe. They help us scale to find better manifestations and thoughts that will work with our current belief system but also help us level it up.

Another area of resistance we can come up against is trying to manifest out of what my friend Christy calls "thirsty" energy. When we manifest from a place of desperation, control, need, or lack, we are manifesting from a low, fearful vibration. *Remember, basement vibes bring basement things.* Part of reducing "thirsty" energy comes from releasing the attachment to needing that desire to happen. Being willing to be okay if it doesn't happen. This part is, again, about trust in the Universe.

Think of putting in an offer on a house you really want. If it's the only house left with all the attributes you desire, you may be manifesting from a place of scarcity rather than abundance and possibility. In this scenario, you might manifest out of fear of not getting it. What vibrational message is fear and lack sending out? It's saying, "I won't be okay if this doesn't happen, and I don't believe there's anything else for me." Think of our image of the ten-story building.

If you need something to complete you and want only that thing, you're eliminating the Universe's divine knowledge of better options. You're blocking your blessings when you narrow in on only one person or situation as the solution to your problems.

If you're in a situation where you've decided only one option can bring you joy, I encourage you to hand over your situation to the Universe. Part of knowing the Universe is knowing even if God doesn't deliver *that* particular thing, person, or experience, it will deliver what is meant for you at this time.

Releasing resistance requires a release of doubt and a release of control. We have to trust that, even though we can intend and manifest, we don't have the final say in what the future holds. We have to trust that the Universe will place the perfect experiences for our optimal growth and happiness in our hands. Remember that bigger blueprint we talked about? Sometimes the Universe has something up its sleeve way better than you might be currently dreaming of. Our job is to stay open to receiving the right thing in our best and highest good, not just the specific thing we've locked in on. A great additive for releasing resistance when you're manifesting is to say, "I'm manifesting this or something better."

In releasing resistance, you have to shift your focus to what you do want rather than what you don't want. The more doubt you have, the less likely you will see it manifest. Finding the best manifestations for you come with exploring and feeling your personal set points. Get honest with yourself about what you are truly willing to believe. Trust that the Universe will give you the right thing at the right time. Plus, our higher power may have something even better up its sleeve you couldn't have dreamed up. Find patience and trust the process. Just a reminder, you don't find out you're pregnant and then get to hold the baby the next day. Good things take time.

Chapter 32:
HOW TO RECEIVE

Now, we don't have to obsessively envision our manifestations. Remember the first time I manifested, set the intention, and forgot about it? We receive most easily when we are open to the belief, taking good care of ourselves, raising our vibration, and can let go of needing what we are asking for. Sounds counterintuitive to ask for something you want, then not need it. But I promise this part can feel like magic.

This part is called surrender. We might catch ourselves ruminating or stressing about something and then decide God's got it. No amount of stress or worry will ever bring better experiences into our life. This is where we can go all the way back to the acceptance we learned in The Part That Feels Dark. Neutral energy is a great attraction point for what we desire. "I don't know what is going to happen next, but I surrender to the Universe to bring what is in my best and highest good."

My favorite way to receive? Put yourself into a high vibration by finding what brings you joy. Dancing around the kitchen with your kiddos? Prime for receiving. Playing catch on the beach with your friends? You're basically an open pathway for God's goodness. Become intentional about your happiness—whether that's being playful, trying a new recipe, learning a meditation practice, or going to a dance class you've never tried before. Maybe it's connecting with a friend who always makes you feel good or listening to good music, podcasts, or YouTube videos. It could be reading a new book or singing a song at the top of your lungs. It could be choosing to forego complaining and instead talk about something that's going well. It can look as simple as finding something to be grateful for. My point? You receive easiest when you can be in the present moment and find a little bit of a better feeling.

Another important way to receive is to keep your energy clear, meaning you can create a routine around your energy that we discussed in the previous chapters. This includes the use of Epsom salt baths, meditation, palo santo, and sage. Cleared and balanced energy also looks like being in alignment by honoring, speaking, and living in your truth. Our energy can get muddied by cognitive dissonance. Alignment, again, is when your thoughts, feelings, and behaviors match. When you're living in alignment, you're a magnet for your desires.

The best way to receive your desire isn't to worry about what might not happen or worst-case scenarios. It's not gossiping with your co-workers about the new girl or griping on Facebook. It's not spending every waking hour manifesting, either. It's finding little moments that bring you joy. Reaching for the next feel-good thought. Making a list of things you love. Relaxing in a bubble bath or writing yourself a love letter. *See, I told you this could be easy.*

Your life is meant to be fun and magical. It's up to you to design it that way. From there, you're a receptor for all things destined for you. The greatest way to become a magnet for your manifestations is to move up the vibrational elevator and find neutrality or joy. Clear your energy. Surrender your worries to the Universe, knowing that if it doesn't deliver what you want, it's because it has a better plan in place. Remember, the Universe is happening for you.

Chapter 33:

WARNING: TOXIC MANIFESTATION

When people first learn about manifesting, they sometimes feel scared of negative emotions and pretend to be happy or optimistic at all times. We're humans, and all emotions, even heavy ones, can be useful guides. Bad feeling emotions often tell us what's not working and what we don't want so we can manifest what does.

If you're avoiding your negative emotions entirely, manifestation can be toxic. We call this positivity bypassing, where we still experience disappointments, resentment, jealousy, or fear but pretend we don't. This doesn't mean we aren't feeling or experiencing negative emotions. It just means we aren't acknowledging it, to be able to move through it, or process to get it out of our mind, heart, and energy field. Instead, we bury it.

Positivity bypassing will create the cognitive dissonance and internal anxiety that we discussed earlier. Holding anxiety in your energy field doesn't put you in place to attract the incredible things you deserve. I recommend honoring, sitting with, and loving up on *all* of your feelings. They are all valid and serve a function. Be honest with yourself. Take care of yourself. Challenge your limiting beliefs and hold compassion for the purpose they have served in your life. Process and clear what bothers you.

Remember, even once you start manifesting, it's okay to hold compassion for a tough day and situation. Talking to a therapist or taking medications that help you feel better is okay, too, when needed. It's okay to doubt yourself or have bad thoughts. In fact, it's normal! It's up to you to lovingly process your harder emotions, not avoid them. Feeling your feels makes space for us to receive more in our life. You may need to go back to the basics at any given time. Our job in working with manifestation is not to pretend bad situations don't exist. Instead, when we can, we seek to remember our power in taking care of ourselves. Clearing our energy and returning to changing our mindset. Manifesting when we are ready. You are not alone. The Universe is on your side waiting to show up for you.

The Ultimate Bad Day Reset:

Step 1: Recognize its a bad day, not a bad life.

Step 2: Hold Compassion for yourself.

Step 3: Move your body.

Step 4: Do an energy reset meditation, use sage, or take an epsom salt bath.

Step 5: Set intentions or Manifest

Step 6: Focus on Fueling Your Body with Food or Water

BONUS: Listen to Jason Stephenson or Michael Sealey while you sleep.

Chapter 34:

SELF-LOVE:
THE KEY TO IT ALL

When I was little, I looked for people to give me the things I needed. I'd wait patiently for approval or validation. I see this now with my kids, too, as they wait for me to praise their artwork or watch a dance they made up. But I've wondered lately: what if when we feel that pull to get something from others, it's just a cue to remember what we need to be actively giving to ourselves? What if before I praised the girls, I asked them how *they* felt about their work? Perhaps the pride and love we look for from the people we care about can first be cultivated within ourselves.

People's opinions are fleeting. The same person who loves us now might hate us later. The same person who hates us now could love us later. I've had some bullies from high school go from slamming me into a locker to promoting my work.

I'm not saying to never rely on people. Connection makes the world go 'round. We need it for survival, but we often prioritize our connection and validation from others over our connection and approval with ourselves. What if we are more careful with us? I want you to ask yourself what you need from anyone outside of you right now. What would you like to hear? How do you wish they would treat you?

What if instead of waiting for the apology for the way someone treated you, you were able to look in the mirror and say, "I am so sorry. You deserve to be treated better." What if the love we so deeply desire, we can give ourselves?

Perhaps the noticing we crave can be gained by some intentional time with just us. What if we take ourselves on dates and adventures? Romanticize our life by making small moments special? Water out of champagne glasses?! Fancy! What if we set out to treat ourselves with such loving intention and care? How would our worlds be different?

We can invite people into our world. We can set standards and give them guidelines to treat us well, but in the end, none of that truly matters if we aren't also treating ourselves well. If we aren't whispering, "Hey hottie, you're doing great," as we get ready in the morning instead of sending hate mail to our stretch marks and cellulite. No outside praise or validation will last if we fail to show up for ourselves.

So, next time you just wish some person would truly see you or love you, ask yourself when the last time you truly saw yourself or loved yourself was? When was the last time you held yourself in high regard? When was the last time you admired your cute quirks and in-between moments? When was the last time you were just so damn proud? Love yourself first—it teaches others how.

One of my favorite practices is to grab a piece of paper. Write down everything you wish another person would say to you, whether from a parent, friend, lover, ex, child, or anyone from whom you've been needing love. Explore the messages. Then write a love note to yourself, including some of those messages and needs. You can even write a love note back in time to the ten-year-old version of you who might have been bullied or neglected. The thirteen-year-old version who had a birthday party no one came to. The twenty-five-year-old version who fell in love with the wrong person. Whatever you need, whatever part of you needs it, now is a perfect time to love yourself.

Although self-love has become a trending movement that glorifies bubble baths and nail painting, it's so much more than that. It's the dirty work. The ugly truth. The honest conversations. It's challenging yourself. Asking more for yourself. It's holding your hand over your heart, tuning into yourself and what you need. It's apologizing and forgiving yourself. It's the way you speak to that inner version of you that just wants to be seen, heard, and loved.

You are worthy of being loved properly. You are worthy of being valued and of having people support you. You are safe. It's okay to trust in something good for yourself. It's okay to believe more is possible. It's okay to want more. And it's okay to go fucking get it for yourself.

Dedicate yourself to small practices of treating yourself with love. Make a habit out of it. When you begin treating yourself like someone you love, that's when it all clicks into place. One of the most miraculous moments is to find a place of love and respect for yourself so deep that no one can mess it up for you. No one's thoughts or opinions matter more than *yours*. That's real power, and luckily, you've had it in you all along.

FINAL THOUGHTS

Typing that out made me feel like the 1990s talk show host Jerry Springer, who always used to say that at the end of his program. And in true Jerry Springer spirit, "Until next time, take care of yourself...and each other."

I've loved this journey with you, and I'm so fucking proud of you. You could've given up on the dark part. Definitely could've flipped me the bird during the questioning and undoing parts. Some of you might still be rolling your eyes at the part in the light. But I hope you feel more powerful than you did when we started. I hope you recognize the innate light in you and your ability to recreate yourself and claim your comeback no matter what has happened in the past.

Whatever stuff came up for you while reading this book, I'm proud of you for continuing anyway. You could've quit. You could've put this baby through a wood-chipper or written me a crappy review on Goodreads. (Please don't!) But you didn't. And that's just one more win to write down in your big book of awesomeness.

You have to have the guts to face your own bullshit. Weak people don't even attempt it. They say, "That's just who I am" while wallowing in their misery and blaming the world for where they are at. But you! You've learned a few things. You've grown.

We will never be perfect. Thank God, because that sounds boring as shit. But we can be authentic and loving and believe bigger for ourselves and our futures. You're a creator, after all. *Stardust, was it?* And your future looks so incredibly bright. Because it gets to be easy. It gets to be fun. Most importantly, it gets to be magic. Welcome to your Comeback. You made it. The power is yours, my dearest friends; choose wisely.

Oh, and I love you. I'm not crying; you're crying.

Xo, Nichole

RESOURCES

Below is a list of some of the books, research studies, and ideas or influencers I studied or drew from in the process of creating this book.

1. "'Reality' Is Constructed by Your Brain. Here's what that Means, and why It Matters." Wu Tsai Neurosciences Institute Stanford University. June 22, 2022. https://neuroscience.stanford.edu/news/reality-constructed-your-brain-here-s-what-means-and-why-it-matters.

2. Suni, Eric. "Mental Health and Sleep." Sleep Foundation. March 17, 2023. https://www.sleepfoundation.org/mental-health.

3. Cooper, Joanna A. "Screens and Your Sleep: The Impact of Nighttime Use." Sutter Health. https://www.sutterhealth.org/health/sleep/screens-and-your-sleep-the-impact-of-nighttime-use.

4. Cortie, Colin H., Mitchell K. Byrne, Carole Collier, Natalie Parletta, Donna Crawford, Pia C. Winberg, David Webster et al. "The Effect of Dietary Supplementation on Aggressive Behaviour in Australian Adult Male Prisoners: A Feasibility and Pilot Study for a Randomised, Double Blind Placebo Controlled

Trial." *Nutrients 12*, no. 9 (2020): 2617. Accessed April 13, 2023. https://doi.org/10.3390/nu12092617.

5. "How Much Protein Do You Need Every Day?" Harvard Health Publishing. January 19, 2022. https://www.health.harvard.edu/blog/how-much-protein-do-you-need-every-day-201506188096#:~:text=The%20Recommended%20Dietary%20Allowance%20(RDA,per%20kilogram%20of%20body%20weight.

6. Zhang, Na, Song M. Du, Jian F. Zhang, and Guan S. Ma. "Effects of Dehydration and Rehydration on Cognitive Performance and Mood among Male College Students in Cangzhou, China: A Self-Controlled Trial." *Int J Environ Res Public Health 16*, no. 11 (2019): 1891. Accessed April 13, 2023. https://doi.org/10.3390/ijerph16111891.

7. Dietrich, Arne. "Transient Hypofrontality as a Mechanism for the Psychological Effects of Exercise." *Psychiatry Research 154*, no. 1 (2006): 79083. Accessed April 13, 2023. https://doi.org/10.1016/j.psychres.2005.07.033.

8. "Using Light (Sunlight, Blue Light & Red Light) to Optimize Health." Andrew Huberman. April 18, 2022. Video, https://www.youtube.com/watch?v=UF0nqolsNZc.

9. Penckofer, Sue, Kouba Joanne, Mary Byrn, and Carol E. Ferrans. "Vitamin D and Depression: Where Is All the Sunshine?" *Issues in Mental Health Nursing 31,* no. 6 (2010): 385-393. Accessed April 13, 2023. https://doi.org/10.3109/01612840903437657.

10. Oschman, James L., Gaétan Chevalier, and Richard Brown. "The Effects of Grounding (Earthing) on Inflammation, the Immune Response, Wound Healing, and Prevention and Treatment of Chronic Inflammatory and Autoimmune Diseases." *Journal of Inflammation Res 8,* (2015): 83-96. Accessed April 13, 2023. https://doi.org/10.2147/JIR.S69656.

11. Kushner, Robert F., and Seung W. Choi. "Prevalence of Unhealthy Lifestyle Patterns among Overweight and Obese Adults." *Obesity 18,* no. 6 (2010): 1160-7. Accessed April 13, 2023. https://doi.org/10.1038/oby.2009.376.

12. Eger, Edith E., and Esme S. Weigand. 2018. *The Choice: Embrace the Possible.* New York: Scribner.

13. "Do You Love YOURSELF or Your LOVER More? | W/ John Kim." Ed Mylett. August 30, 2022. Video, https://www.youtube.com/watch?v=Cnnktx1fAu0.

14. Nelson, Dana. "Self-Care 101: Setting Healthy Boundaries." Inner Journeys Counseling. December 8, 2106. http://www.dananelsoncounseling.com/blog/self-care-setting-healthy-boundaries/.

15. Levine, Amir, and Rachel Heller. 2012. *Attached: The New Science of Adult Attachment and How It Can Help You Find—and Keep—Love*. New York: TarcherPerigee.

16. Skinner, B. F., and C. B. Ferster. 1957. *Schedules of Reinforcement*. New York: Appleton-Century-Crofts. https://doi.org/10.1037/10627-000.

17. Tsent, Julie, and Jordan Poppenk. "Brain Meta-state Transitions Demarcate Thoughts Across Task Contexts Exposing the Mental Noise of Trait Neuroticism." *Nat Commun 11*, no. 1 (2020): 3480. Accessed April 13, 2023. https://doi.org/10.1038/s41467-020-17255-9.

18. Frank, Britt. 2022. *The Science of Stuck: Breaking Through Inertia to Find Your Path Forward*. New York: TarcherPerigee.

19. Grout, Pam. 2013. *E-Squared: Nine Do-It-Yourself Energy Experiments That Prove Your Thoughts Create Your Reality*. 5th ed. Hay House Insights.

20. "Using Play to Rewire & Improve Your Brain | Huberman Lab Podcast #58." Andrew Huberman. February 7, 2022. Video, https://www.youtube.com/watch?v=BwyZIWeBpRw.

21. Thorpe, Matthew, and Rachael Ajmera. "12 Science-Based Benefits of Meditation." Healthline. October

27, 2020. https://www.healthline.com/nutrition/12-benefits-of-meditation.

22. Ranganathan, Vinoth K., Vlodek Siemionow, Jing Z. Liu, Vinod Saghal, and Guang H. Yue. "From Mental Power to Muscle Power—Gaining Strength by Using the Mind." *Neuropsychologia 42*, no. 7 (2004): 944-956. Accessed April 13, 2023. https://doi.org/10.1016/j.neuropsychologia.2003.11.018.

23. Steel, Craig, Kees Korrelbloom, M Fazil Baksh, Judit Simon, Til Wykes, Peter Phiri, and Mark van der Gaag. "Positive Memory Training for the Treatment of Depression in Schizophrenia: A Randomised Controlled Trial." *Behav Res Ther. 135*, (2020). Accessed April 13, 2023. https://doi.org/10.1016/j.brat.2020.103734.

24. Carney, Dana R., Amy J. C. Cuddy, and Andy J. Yap. "Power Posing: Brief Nonverbal Displays Affect Neuroendocrine Levels and Risk Tolerance." *Psychology Science* no. 10 (2010): 1363-8. Accessed April 13, 2023. https://doi.org/10.1177/0956797610383437.

25. Carney, Dana R., Amy J. C. Cuddy, and Andy J. Yap. "Power Posing: Brief Nonverbal Displays Affect Neuroendocrine Levels and Risk Tolerance." *Psychology Science* no. 10 (2010): 1363-8. Accessed April 13, 2023. https://doi.org/10.1177/0956797610383437.

26. Borowski, Susan. "Quantum Mechanics and the Consciousness Connection." AAAS. July 16, 2012. https://www.aaas.org/quantum-mechanics-and-consciousness-connection.

27. Gladwell, Malcolm. 2019. *Talking to Strangers: What We Should Know about the People We Don't Know*. Little, Brown and Company.

28. "Press Release." The Nobel Prize. The Royal Swedish Academy of Sciences, October 4, 2022. https://www.nobelprize.org/prizes/physics/2022/press-release/.

29. "Rethinking Death to Understand Life." Gabriela Reyes Fuchs. Video, https://www.ted.com/talks/gabriela_reyes_fuchs_repensar_la_muerte_para_entender_la_vida?language=en.

30. "The Elements of Life Mapped Across the Milky Way by SDSS/APOGEE." SDSS. January 5, 2017. https://www.sdss.org/press-releases/the-elements-of-life-mapped-across-the-milky-way-by-sdssapogee/.

31. Moncrieff, Joanna, Ruth E. Cooper, Tom Stockmann, Simone Amendola, Michael P. Hengartner, and Mark A. Horowitz. "The Serotonin Theory of Depression: A Systematic Umbrella Review of the Evidence." *Molecular Psychiatry*, (2022): 1-14. Accessed April 17, 2023. https://www.nature.com/articles/s41380-022-01661-0.

32. Huberman, Andrew. "@hubermanlab." Instagram. July 25, 2022. https://www.instagram.com/hubermanlab/.

33. Mansuy, Isabel M., and Safa Mohanna. "Epigenetics and the Human Brain: Where Nurture Meets Nature." *Cerebrum* 8, (2011). Accessed April 17, 2023. https://pubmed.ncbi.nlm.nih.gov/23447777/.

34. James, Karin H., and Laura Engelhardt. "The Effects of Handwriting Experience on Functional Brain Development in Pre-literate Children." *Trends in Neuroscience and Education 1*, no. 1 (2009): 32-42. Accessed April 17, 2023. https://doi.org/10.1016/j.tine.2012.08.001.

35. "Lady Gaga | On The Record." Fuse. March 11, 2012. Video, https://www.youtube.com/watch?v=NJ5UQOMlEQo.

FURTHER RECOMMENDED READING

Books

A Course in Miracles: Combined Volume by Foundation for Inner Peace

Atomic Habits: Tiny Changes, Remarkable Results: An Easy and Proven Way to Build Good Habits and Break Bad Ones by James Clear

Becoming Supernatural: How Common People Are Doing the Uncommon by Joe Dispenza and Gregg Braden

Believe Bigger: Discover the Path to Your Life Purpose by Marshawn Evans Daniels

A Theory of Cognitive Dissonance by Leon Festinger

How to Do the Work: Recognize Your Patterns, Heal from Your Past, and Create Your Self by Nicole Lepera

Not Another Diet Book: A Guide to Learning to Listen to and Honor Your Body by Heather Maio

Articles

"Mirror Neurons: From Origin to Function" by Richard Cook, Geoffrey Bird, Caroline Catmur, Clare Press, and Ceclia Hayes

"What Happened to Mirror Neurons" by Caroline Catmur and Cecila Hayes

"You Are Hardwired to Survive: How Your Brain Has Evolved to Be the Ultimate Survivor" by P.J. Kieger

"Amino Acid and Protein Requirements: Cognitive Performance, Stress, and Brain Function" by Harris R. Lieberman

"The Scientific Reason Your Perception Creates Your Reality" by James McCrae

"Neurotheology: Are We Hardwired for God?" by René Muller

"The Structure and Consequences of Repetitive Thought: How What's on Your Mind, and How, and How Much, Affects Your Health" by Suzanne Segerstrom

"Your Brain on Imagination: It's a Lot like Reality, Study Shows" by University of Colorado at Boulder

Influencers

Abraham Hicks, author of *Ask and It Is Given*

Amanda Frances, author of *Rich as F*ck*, self-proclaimed "money queen," and thought leader on financial empowerment for women

Amy Shah, gut health expert and author of *I'm So Effing Tired: A Proven Plan to Beat Burnout, Boost Your Energy, and Reclaim Your Life*

Andrew Huberman, neuroscientist and host of the Huberman Lab Podcast

Anna Runkle, creator of the Crappy Childhood Fairy YouTube channel

B.F. Skinner, American behavioral psychologist who produced the idea of intermittent reinforcement conditioning

Ed Mylett host of the podcast the Ed Mylett Show, author of *The Power of One More*

Edith Eger, clinical psychologist and author of *The Choice: Embrace the Possible*

Gabby Bernstein, motivational speaker specializing in spirituality and author of *Spirit Junkie*

Gabrielle Reyes Fuchs, 2018 TedX speaker of "Rethinking Death to Understand Life"

Joe Dispenza, scientist, author *Becoming Supernatural: How Common People Are Doing the Uncommon*

John Kim, licensed therapist, life coach, host of "The Angry Therapist" podcast, author of *It's Not Me, It's You*

Max Planck, Nobel Prize-winning physicist known for discovering quantum theory

Oprah Winfrey, American talk show host, television producer, actress, author, and philanthropist

Wayne Dyer, spirituality speaker and self-help author of *I Can See Clearly Now*

Ideas

Cognitive psychology: Although there are many psychologists to credit in the development of cognitive psychology, Ulric Neisser is considered the "father" of the movement, interweaving research to gain a better understanding of internal processing, patterns, attention, and problem-solving.

Maslow's Hierarchy of Needs: Proposed by psychologist Abraham Maslow in 1943, Maslow's Hierarchy of Needs suggests that individuals intrinsically find behavioral motivation. Sustaining the bottom layers of the pyramid suggest that you can more quickly and easily move up the scale toward self-actualization. More information is available at simplypsychology.com.

Programs

The 12 Step Program is a group designed to help people quit or abstain from drugs, alcohol, or addictions.

Al-Anon is a group designed to help those who have friends or relatives who have currently or in the past been addicted to a substance.

YouTube Suggestions

Michael Sealey: https://www.youtube.com/c/Michael Sealey

Jason Stephenson: https://www.youtube.com/c/Jason StephensonSleepMeditationMusic

ACKNOWLEDGMENTS

Writing a book is quite the process. An introspective one that feels like you're all alone but somehow involves a million other people who are there to remind you, you're not alone. I'm forever grateful for the people who supported me in writing this book.

Brandon – I was 17 when I told you I wanted to be a writer someday. You responded by buying me a laptop when you worked a part-time job at a retail store and had no money. You believed in me from the start. Your unwavering belief in me is the reason this book exists. Thank you for supporting me, guiding me, and trusting me to invest in myself and my dreams. I love you.

Samantha – From the electric slide in third grade to grown-ups who almost, kind of, sort of, have their shit together. Thank you for cheering me on, reading a million versions of this, and for your incredible friendship over the years. I have no idea what I would do without you.

Natasha – Your divine editing skills have fine-tuned and elevated this book into something I am deeply proud of. Thank you for taking a chance on some random girl off Instagram. I can't thank you enough.

Penny – Thank you for being so supportive. Having every month at the top of your calendar pose the question, "Is Nichole's book getting released this month?" since July 2022. Guess what?! It's finally here!

Christy – Thank you for always yielding my questions and amplifying my own intuition and reminding me it's safe to be myself.

Heather – Thank you for giving me the space to obsess about every process in my book. For being the best co-host a gal could ask for. So lucky we met!

Liz – Thank you for celebrating every milestone with me. For always leaving space for my meltdowns. For swooping in with mid-day mimosas when needed.

My Readers – A book without being read is just a doorstopper. You could've picked any book on the shelf, but you chose this one. You are what makes the writing come into action and brings my dreams to life. I'm forever grateful for each and every one of you.

ABOUT THE AUTHOR

Nichole Eaton is an intuitive therapist, two-time author, host of the *Rock Your Comeback* podcast, and creator of The Comeback Club. Nichole has brought dynamic transformation to thousands of clients with her unique style that interweaves her unique experience as both a mental health counselor and an intuitive. Nichole has a true passion for helping others find their purpose, break through blocks, and reconnect with their personal power.

KEEP UP WITH NICHOLE

Join the Comeback Club:
https://nicholeeaton.com/pages/the-comeback-club

Instagram:
www.instagram.com/NicholeEaton.xo

TikTok:
www.tiktok.com/nicholeeaton.xo

Learn more or book a service with Nichole at:
www.nicholeeaton.com

Subscribe to Nichole's *Rock Your Comeback* podcast on Spotify, Apple Podcasts, and just about everywhere podcasts are played.

CREATING DISTINCTIVE BOOKS
WITH INTENTIONAL RESULTS

We're a collaborative group of creative masterminds
with a mission to produce high-quality books to position
you for monumental success in the marketplace.

Our professional team of writers, editors, designers,
and marketing strategists work closely together to ensure
that every detail of your book is a clear representation
of the message in your writing.

Want to know more?

Write to us at info@publishyourgift.com
or call (888) 949-6228

Discover great books, exclusive offers, and more at
www.PublishYourGift.com

Connect with us on social media

@publishyourgift

Printed in the USA
CPSIA information can be obtained
at www.ICGtesting.com
JSHW011802100823
46333JS00007B/29

9 781644 846261